collections

Houghton Mifflin Harcourt

Close Reader

GRADE 9

Program Consultants:

Kylene Beers

Martha Hougen

Carol Jago

William L. McBride

Erik Palmer

Lydia Stack

Cover, Title Page Photo Credits: ©Marc Guitierrez/Getty Images

Printed in the U.S.A.

ISBN 978-0-544-08769-9

13 14 15 0690 19 18 17

4500647441   B C D E F G

fyi hmhfyi.com **Visit hmhfyi.com** for current articles and informational texts.

COLLECTION 3
The Bonds Between Us

COLLECTION 4
Sweet Sorrow

© Houghton Mifflin Harcourt Publishing Company • Image Credits: ©Carlos Sanchez Pereyra/Alamy Images; ©Sandy MacKenzie/Shutterstock

COLLECTION 5

A Matter of Life or Death

COLLECTION 6

Heroes and Quests

visit FYI.com
for current articles and information texts.
hmhfyi.com

Becoming A Close Reader

READING THE TEXTS

Challenging literary and informational texts require close reading to understand and appreciate their meanings fully. These texts may have difficult language or complex structures that become clear only with careful study. To fully understand these demanding texts, you need to learn how to read and reread slowly and deliberately.

The Close Reader provides many opportunities to practice close reading. To become a close reader,

- read each text in the Close Reader slowly all the way through.
- take time to think about and respond to the READ and REREAD prompts that help focus your reading.
- cite specific textual evidence to support your analysis of the selection.

Your goal in close reading is to build useful knowledge as you analyze the author's message and appreciate the author's craft.

Within the textbook page image:

Background Eboo Patel believes that religion should bring people together. Inspired by both his Muslim faith and his Indian heritage, he founded the Interfaith Youth Core with a Jewish friend in Chicago in 2002 and later served on President Obama's Advisory Council on Faith-based and Neighborhood Partnerships. This essay is from his Washington Post blog The Faith Divide. This entry was adapted from his Freshman Convocation Address at George Washington University on the tenth anniversary of 9/11.

Making the Future Better, Together

Blog by Eboo Patel

1. **READD** As you read lines 1–21, begin to collect and cite text evidence.
   - Underline the two situations Patel is comparing.
   - Circle the words Patel thinks define the "essence of our nation."

I thought about George Washington when I was at the airport this weekend, watching women in Islamic headscarves brave the stares and scowls of some of their fellow Americans on an anniversary no one will ever forget.

I wonder if a similar feeling prompted Moses Sessius, the leader of the Hebrew Congregation of Newport, Rhode Island to write George Washington a letter shortly after he assumed the Presidency. It was a letter essentially asking whether Sessius and his people—Jews—would be safe in this new nation, or if they would be hounded and hated, blamed for crimes they did not commit.

In his response, Washington put on paper words that I think still define the essence of our nation:

"The Government of the United States . . . gives to bigotry no sanction, to persecution no assistance, requires only that they who live under its protection should **demean** themselves as good citizens."

demean:

3

CLOSE READ Notes

cynical:

King knew this. But it neither paralyzed him nor made him **cynical**. He didn't tie himself into knots trying to untie that mother of all contradictions. Instead, he committed himself, body and soul, to shaping the future.

America's genius is to give its diversity of citizens a stake in the well-being of the nation. That's what keeps us facing forward, seeking inspiration from the past when possible, correcting mistakes when necessary. This nation could well have been a house divided, but today we stand as one—and that has everything to do with how a previous generation, led by Abraham Lincoln, acted. This nation could easily have been declared a lie by an entire race of people—kidnapped and enslaved, separated out and hunted down. Instead King and his movement termed it a broken promise, one that the people on the receiving end of the breach took actions to mend.

As a nation, we've spent the last several weeks trying to decipher the meaning of 9/11. That's as it should be; those who were lost on that day deserve that and much much more.

As I looked out at the Freshman Class at George Washington University on the 10th Anniversary of 9/11, they represented for me the next ten years, and the decades after. Here was my message to them:

6. **REREAD** Reread lines 46–64. What point about change was Martin Luther King, Jr. making by telling the story of Rip Van Winkle? Support your answer with explicit textual evidence.

6

Background
This paragraph provides information about the text you are about to read. It helps you understand the context of the selection through additional information about the author, the subject, or the time period in which the text was written.

READ ▶

With practice, you can learn how to be a close reader. Questions and specific instructions at the beginning of the selection and on the bottom of the pages will guide your close reading of each text.

These questions and instructions

- refer to specific sections of the text.
- ask you to look for and mark up specific information in the text.
- prompt you to record inferences and text analysis in the side margins.
- help you begin to collect and cite text evidence.

Vocabulary
Critical vocabulary words appear in the margin throughout most selections. Consult a print or online dictionary to define the word on your own.

When you see a vocabulary word in the margin,

- write the definition of each vocabulary word in the margin.
- be sure your definition fits the context of the word as it is used in the text.
- check your definition by substituting it in place of the vocabulary word from the text. Your definition should make sense in the context of the selection.

◀ REREAD

To further guide your close reading, REREAD questions at the bottom of the page will

- ask you to focus on a close analysis of a smaller chunk of text.
- prompt you to analyze literary elements and devices, as well as the meaning and structure of informational text.
- help you go back into the text and "read between the lines" to uncover possible meanings and central ideas.

CLOSE READ
Notes

When you are wronged, in ways both small and large, remember what Martin Luther King Jr. said in the waning days of the Montgomery Bus Boycott, after the African-Americans of that city had endured a year of walking to work, of facing false arrests and very real death threats, King gave a speech about looking forward, about building the nation: "Now is the time for redemption, now is the time for reconciliation, now is the time to build the beloved community."

9. ◀ REREAD AND DISCUSS Reread lines 80–97. In the margin of lines 91–97, summarize King's hopes. Then, with a small group, discuss the kind of world Patel envisions for the future.

SHORT RESPONSE

Cite Text Evidence Explain whether or not Patel convinced you that the United States is a nation that cherishes its diversity. Review your reading notes, and evaluate the effectiveness of the examples and evidence. Be sure to cite text evidence from the blog in your response.

8

◀ REREAD AND DISCUSS

These prompts encourage you to work with a partner or in a small group to discuss specific events, details, statements, and evidence from the text. These discussions will allow you to acquire and share knowledge about the texts you are reading.

As you engage in these discussions,

- be sure to cite specific text evidence in support of your statements.
- pose questions and integrate your ideas with the ideas of others.
- collaborate to reach a consensus or call attention to evidence that might have been missed or misinterpreted.
- acknowledge the views of others and be ready to modify your own thinking.

SHORT RESPONSE

At the end of each text, you will have an opportunity to sum up your thinking by completing a Short Response. The Short Response represents a place to convey some of the ideas you have developed through close reading of the text.

When you write your Short Response,

- review all of your margin notes and REREAD answers.
- circle or highlight evidence from your notes that supports your position or point of view.
- clearly state your point of view and support it with reasons.
- cite specific text evidence to support your reasons.

Finding Common Ground

Finding Common Ground

"We may have different religions, different languages, different colored skin, but we all belong to one human race."

—Kofi Annan

Background Lisa Fugard *grew up in South Africa, the daughter of the playwright and actor Athol Fugard and Sheila Fugard, a novelist and poet. Fugard came to the United States in 1980 and worked as an actress before she turned to writing. The following story is set in South Africa, though the red-crested heron Fugard describes does not actually exist.*

Night Calls

Short Story by Lisa Fugard

CLOSE READ
Notes

1. **READD ▷** As you read lines 1–26, begin to collect and cite text evidence.

    • Underline text that describes the narrator's father.
    • Circle text that hints at the narrator's feelings toward her father.

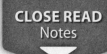

My father's hands were huge. Slablike. When he was idle, they seemed to hang off the ends of his arms like two chunks of meat. He sat on his hands during the months he courted my mother.

When I was thirteen, I watched my thin hand disappear into his. It was at the train station at Modder River. I'd come home for the September holidays. It was hot, and the only other car at the small station pulled away. The siding at Modder River, 150 miles north of Johannesburg, was never busy. I remember it all clearly, standing in the dust, watching him get out of the truck and walk toward me, noticing that there was no smile on his face but still feeling my body move toward him, my arms opening for an embrace, something rising in my throat. My father stopped and held out his right hand.

Once in the truck, I was filled with anxiety about how close to him I could sit. I settled in the middle of my half of the bench seat and watched his large, brown hand move from the steering wheel to the gearshift and back. I breathed deeply. Suddenly I was filled with the smell of him:

10

Borkum Riff tobacco, sweat, the sweet odor of cheap Cape brandy. Filled with his secrets, I felt like a thief and moved a little closer to the window.

Then we were at the entrance to the Modder River Wildlife Sanctuary, and I jumped out of the car to open the gate. It swung easily, once I unlatched it, and banged against the wooden fence post, startling several guinea fowl that scampered into the veld.[1] "Krrdll . . . krrdll . . . krrdll," I called, and they slowed down. I mimicked their rattling cry again, and they stopped. Again, and a few of them stepped hesitantly toward me. Laughingly, I turned to find my father's smile, but his face was gone, blotted out by the expanse of blue sky reflected in the windshield.

I have a gift for mimicking bird and animal calls. During my third year at boarding school I'd finally made myself popular and gained the respect of Wendy Venter, the bully of our dorm, by doing several calls late one night. It became a ritual, and every couple of weeks, around midnight, I'd hear rustling and whispering from the eleven other girls in the dormitory; then a balled-up sock would land on my bed, usually right next to my head, and Wendy would call my name in a sly whisper, "Marlene." The dorm would fall silent. Lying back in the darkness I'd start with the deep moan of the spotted eagle owl; then the high-pitched yip of the black-backed jackal; the low snuffle and violent laugh of the hyena; and then a deadly combination: the rasping, half-swallowed growl of the leopard, followed by the wild scream of the chacma baboon. Inevitably one of the younger girls would begin to cry, and I'd hear Wendy snickering in the darkness.

I'd told my father about this during my next trip home, about how much the other girls had enjoyed it, and I offered to do it for him one evening, offered to steal into his room at midnight, crouch at the foot of his bed, and make the calls for him. He'd shaken his head ever so slightly. "I've got the real thing right outside my window," he said.

As we drove up to our house now, I noticed the shabby state of the compound. The road was rutted and washed-out in many places by the spring rains. The visitors' kiosk was boarded up, and the map of the sanctuary had been knocked off its post and lay on the ground. Even the

---

[1] **veld:** in South Africa, open grassy country with few bushes and almost no trees.

2. **◄ REREAD** Reread lines 4–12 and lines 19–26. In the margins, explain what the narrator wants from her father and what she gets instead.

3. **READ ▷** As you read lines 27–44, continue to cite textual evidence.

- Circle the reason why the narrator describes her ability to mimic bird and animal calls "a gift."
- Underline her father's response to her calls.

pond had been neglected. When my parents had first come to Modder
50 River, five years before I was born, my father had had the pond dug out for
my mother. An avid botanist,[2] she'd planted it with indigenous water lilies
that she collected, along with bulrushes, seven-weeks ferns, and floating
hearts. During the two years when the Modder River was reduced to a
trickle by the drought, the local farmers had been astonished to hear that
my father was actually pumping precious water from our borehole into the
pond to prevent it from drying up. An **opulent** jewel in the dusty, cracked
landscape, it became a haven for birds, being visited by pied kingfishers,
mountain chats, spoonbills, bokmakieries, a pair of black-shouldered
kites—all told, my mother counted 107 different species. Now a thick layer
60 of brown scum covered the shallow, stagnant water. I remembered a letter
that I'd received from my father several months before. The scrawled
handwriting hadn't even looked like his. I'd read it once and then hidden it
away, scared by the loneliness that the words hinted at.

    None of this seemed to matter, however, when I stood among our dogs,
being pelted with paws and tails and long pink tongues: King, with his tail
plumed like an ostrich feather, and Blitz, a lean, black shadow. They
clattered behind me as I went into my bedroom. The room was still and
dark and smelled musty. Quickly I opened the wooden shutters. I moved to
the chest of drawers and found the large framed photograph of my mother,
70 frozen at age thirty-two. She was laughing, and her head was turned slightly
as a lock of hair blew across her face. I traced her jaw line with my finger
and moved to the mirror with the photograph, but the dogs were
demanding, barking and pawing at my legs.

    I ran outside with them and chased them up and down the cool stone
lengths of the veranda, flying past the living room and the dining room,
screeching past my father's study and back again with the dogs racing
behind me. Back and forth I went, until the force of motion made me round
the corner past my parents' old bedroom. I stopped, panting, trying to catch
my breath. I stared at the large fenced-in area under the blue gum tree. It

---

[2] **botanist:** a scientist who studies plant life.

opulent:

4. **◀ REREAD** Reread lines ?1–44. In the margin, make an inference
   about how the narrator probably felt about her father's response to her
   new talent.

5. **READ ▶** As you read lines 45–94, underline details that describe how
   the compound at Modder River has changed. Circle words that describe
   changes in Marlene's father.

80 was where my father kept the red-crested night heron, one of the last of its
kind.

The year that the park officials brought the bird to Modder River had
been a difficult one. My mother was killed in a car accident just before my
eighth birthday. Numbly, I watched my father make funeral arrangements
with the help of his sister, Annette, who drove up from Johannesburg. She
was adamant: There was no way I could stay at Modder River. It was too
remote, and there was my schooling to consider; my mother had been my
tutor. As for my father, it made no sense for him to remain, grieving, in a
place so closely associated with his wife. My father was on the verge of
90 resigning as warden of the small sanctuary when park officials telephoned
about the bird. The red-crested night heron had been captured at the vlei³
on Nie Te Ver, the farm abutting the sanctuary's eastern border, and the
National Parks Board wanted the heron kept at Modder River on the slim
chance that they might find a mate for it.

A Mr. Vanjaarsveld arrived with the bird. "We had to tie the bugger's
beak up, otherwise he'd have cut us to ribbons," he said, as he placed a large
burlap bag in the pen that my father had hastily constructed. He opened the
bag and then quickly stepped out and shut the gate. A few moments of
silence—then a wild flurry of wings, the sound of the air being thumped,
100 and the heron hit the wire at the top of the pen and came crashing down.
Again and again, till the bird lay in the dust exhausted, its wings useless.
Quietly my father opened the gate and stepped inside the pen. For several
minutes he squatted on his haunches in the corner and then slowly he
inched his way toward the bird. Kneeling alongside it, he checked the
feathers for damage, spreading the wings on the ground in front of him, like
a fan. Then, making soft noises in the back of his throat, he untied the strip
of burlap around the heron's beak. My father stayed on at Modder River,
and arrangements were made for me to go to boarding school.

_____
³ **vlei:** in South Africa, a temporary lake formed in a marshy area during the rainy season.

6. **◄ REREAD** Reread lines 82–94. The narrator describes the year as
"difficult." In the margin, explain in your own words what happened.

7. **READ ▶** As you read lines 95–139, continue to cite textual evidence.

• Underline the changes the heron brought to Modder River.
• Circle text that describes the heron and its surroundings.

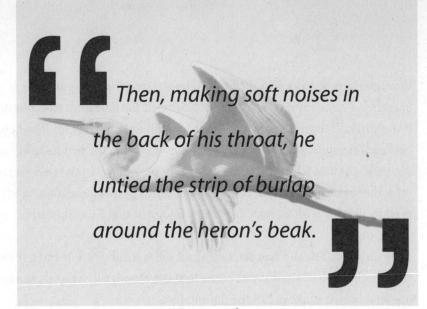

Then, making soft noises in the back of his throat, he untied the strip of burlap around the heron's beak.

During holidays I came home, and my father would share the latest
110   news about the heron with me. He showed me articles from the local papers
lauding the conservation efforts surrounding the bird, as well as articles
from foreign countries in languages we couldn't understand. He showed me
the stamp that the South African government issued—a thirty-seven-cent
stamp with the heron's lean profile and brilliant crest. And once he gave me
a feather, a long, steel-gray feather from the tip of the heron's wing, a flight
feather, and it was smooth as I stroked it against my cheek during the
overnight train ride back to boarding school. But after two or three years,
interest in the heron faded. The articles died down, and in private the
National Parks Board expressed their doubts to my father that they would
120   ever find a mate for the bird. The sanctuary was small, and apart from a
secretive leopard we didn't have any of the Big Five—animals like elephants
and lions that attracted tourists. Modder River returned to the way it used
to be, a trickle of visitors on the occasional weekend.

    I stared at the pen for a long time now. I knew what was in there. A
large gray bird, with ugly hooked feet, a long slithery neck that gave me
nightmares, and a red crest that was raised during the courtship ritual. I
had never seen the crest, but once I'd caught a glimpse of a small red feather
that had escaped from the heron's crown. There was no need to walk

lauding:

8. **◄ REREAD** Reread lines 109–136. In the margin, explain what the
heron might symbolize.

130 through the dust to look at the bird under the swaying blue gum tree branches. I went anyway. Effortlessly, I climbed the blue gum tree, but now it was difficult for me to squeeze into the small fork halfway up. The heron pecked listlessly at a dried-out fish, and I noticed that the pen hadn't been cleaned in quite a while. I'd spent many school holidays in the tree watching my father as he fed the bird, collected the feathers during the molt,[4] and proudly chatted with visitors. Maybe he'd known that I was up there all the time.

I shivered. The sun had set, taking all the warmth with it, and a thin veil of light pressed against our house and the Modder River as it crawled like a fat brown snake out of the mountains.

140 Walking back down the length of the veranda, I peered through the windows of the rooms we'd stopped using, the dining room with its yellow wood table, the living room where my mother's desk was still piled high with the field guides and books she'd used to identify unknown plants she'd come across. The outside light flickered on, and I found my father in the kitchen, heating up a tin of curry. We ate our dinner in silence, and then he read a book and I listened to the radio. I felt uncomfortable in the house and longed for the morning, when I could go racing through the veld with the dogs, go out looking for tracks and walk far into the sanctuary. At 10 P.M., as was custom, my father switched off the electricity generator and 150 went to his study, where he slept.

The low hum now gone, I lay in bed and let the night overtake me, hungrily following the calls in the darkness. A jackal marking his territory, the rhythmic eruptions of spring bullfrogs, the steady breath of King at the foot of my bed. And then I heard another familiar sound, the creaking of the gate on the heron's pen. Gently I felt my way down the hall and into my parents' old bedroom. I hid behind the soft lace curtains, and as my eyes grew accustomed to the night, I saw my father move slowly across the compound carrying the heron gently under his arm, its long legs dangling at his side. The heron's neck was liquid in the moonlight, curving and 160 swaying, at times seeming to entwine my father. Its beak glinted like a

---

[4] **molt:** shedding of feathers at certain intervals, prior to replacement by new growth.

9. **READ ▶** As you read lines 140–179, underline language that describes how the father seems to be changing. Make notes in the margin in lines 140–150 about what hasn't changed.

14

dagger. One of my father's hands followed the bird's neck, lightly touching it at times, while the other was sunk deep into the heron's soft breast, pale, gray feathers around his wrist. My father slipped by with the heron, and I went back to bed and stared into the darkness. Later on I heard a **tremulous** wail repeated several times. It came from the river. I knew it was the red-crested night heron, even though I'd never heard its call before, and I thought about my father in the darkness on the banks of the Modder River with the bird.

tremulous:

170   At breakfast the next morning, my father told me that a hyena had gotten the best of us, had finally broken into the heron's pen, because the bird had disappeared. Under the blue gum tree we examined a huge hole in the fence. "Yes, I think so, Dad," I said, and nodded in agreement as we watched King and Blitz sniff inside the pen. He seemed lighter and chatted with me about school as I helped him dismantle the fence. "Hyena," he had said with such authority. He told me that now he might even be able to come to the end-of-the-year recital at my school. That night I made fried bananas and ice cream for dessert, and we listened to a radio play together. At ten, just before he switched off the generator, I looked in the mirror and thought, I have his eyes.

180   In bed, in the blackness, I listened to the night again. The jackal that had been barking the previous night had moved on, and it seemed quiet out there. It wasn't long before I heard the heron calling. I knew my father heard it as well, and I tried to picture him in his bed. I wondered if his heart beat like mine, an urgent knocking in my chest. I rolled over and thought of the red-crested night heron, alone by the river, the last of its kind, and I imagined that its crest was raised and that it picked its way delicately through the muddy water, lifting its feet up like wet handkerchiefs.

The following night I heard the heron's call again, and I also heard footsteps leaving our house. I knew it was my father going down to the
190   river. For ten nights the heron called and my father followed. During the days we worked on repairing things around the compound. We cleaned up the pond and made a day trip to the western corner of the sanctuary, where the Modder River dropped abruptly into a densely forested ravine—gnarled trees hung with a thick gray moss that I called "old man's beard." We

10. **READ** ▶ As you read lines 180–205, circle the unfolding events.

collected water lilies from the dappled pools, wrapping their roots in damp newspaper and placing them in our packs. Baboons barked from the rocky ledges. We saw the spoor of the leopard, two pugmarks[5] in the rich black mud. For the drive home I sat in the back of the truck. As my father shifted to low gear and negotiated the sandy part of the road that ran alongside the
200   river, I scanned the banks, hoping to catch a glimpse of the heron roosting, waiting for nightfall. I spent a day repairing the signs along the Succulent Trail, a one-mile loop that wound through an area that my father had filled with rare plants—aloe albida, aloe monotropa, a lydenberg cycad. We put the map back on its post and touched it up with small pots of paint, the Modder River a blue vein in the brown landscape.

    Then, one long night, I didn't hear the heron's call. The bird had disappeared, and when I got out of bed the next morning, I saw that my father's eyes had gone dull like a dead animal's. I knew why but couldn't say anything. Then he started walking all the time, often coming home only for
210   an hour or two in the early dawn. I'd hear the creak of the floorboards near the kitchen and the thud of Blitz's tail on the floor. I'd hear my father pacing, and then, eventually, stillness. He's lying on the sofa in his study, he's asleep now, I'd say to myself. Then the pacing again and the soft slam of the screen door. From the blue gum tree I'd see him crisscrossing the veld, like a rabid dog, always coming back to touch the river. Straining my eyes, I'd watch him walk farther and farther away, until he vanished into the landscape.

---

[5] **spoor … pugmarks:** *Spoor* is the track or trail of a wild animal. *Pugmarks* are the footprints or trail of an animal.

11. ◀ REREAD   Reread lines 169–205. In the margin, explain how Marlene's relationship with her father has changed. What is her father doing at night? Support your answer with explicit textual evidence.

_____

_____

_____

12. READ ▶   As you read lines 206–231, continue to cite textual evidence.

• Circle language that describes the father in lines 206–217.

• In the margin, make an inference about what the bird might mean to the father.

Accidentally, I found the heron's remains. I was out late one afternoon, looking for a snakeskin for my next school biology project. I had chosen a

220   rocky area, where I'd seen cobras and puff adders sunning themselves, and as I moved slowly through it, poking into crevices with a stick, I came across a broken fan of bloodied feathers. The steel-gray patina was unmistakable, and I knew it was part of the heron's wing. I scratched out a hole with my stick and buried the feathers, pushing a large rock over the small grave.

I made sandwiches for supper that night. I made extra ones for my father, but he didn't come home. I sat on the veranda with King and Blitz until ten o'clock, when I switched off the generator. Swiftly, silently, I

13. **◀ REREAD** Reread lines 218–225. In the margin, explain what happened to the heron. Why does the narrator bury it?

followed the footpath down to the far bank of the river, pushing my way
230 through the warm water that came up to my waist. I hid in the reeds and
waited.

An hour later I saw my father on the opposite bank, looking, listening.
He sat down on the dark sand and rolled a pebble in his large palms. I
crouched even lower. Slowly I tilted my head back until my throat was wide
open and a tremulous wail slid out. My father stood up and looked across
the water to where I was crouched. Again I made the sound, again and
again. He took three more small steps toward my side of the river and his
hands fluttered like giant, tawny moths in the moonlight.

14. **READ ▶** Read lines 232–238. Underline text describing Marlene's
action and her father's response. What does she do, and why? Support
your answer with explicit textual evidence.

_____

_____

_____

SHORT RESPONSE

Cite Text Evidence Think about Marlene's relationship with her father
and what it reveals about the story's theme. Review your reading notes. Be
sure to **cite text evidence** to explain your response.

_____

_____

_____

_____

_____

_____

_____

_____

The Struggle for Freedom

COLLECTION 2
The Struggle for Freedom

"If there is no struggle, there is no progress."

—Frederick Douglass

SPEECH
A Eulogy for
Dr. Martin Luther King Jr.   Robert F. Kennedy

SHORT STORY
The Prisoner Who Wore Glasses   Bessie Head

The Bonds Between Us

The Bonds Between Us

"The welfare of each of us is dependent fundamentally upon the welfare of all of us."

—Theodore Roosevelt

Background *On November 13, 1985, the long-dormant Nevado del Ruiz volcano erupted in Colombia, South America. Molten rock and hot gases melted the volcano's thick ice cap and sent deadly mudslides down its slopes. More than 23,000 people died in the disaster—most of them in the town of Armero. The media focused a lot of attention on one thirteen-year-old girl named Omayra Sánchez who was trapped in the mud.* **Isabel Allende** *uses these facts as the basis for this work of fiction. In her story, the trapped girl is named Azucena, and the man who attempts to rescue her is journalist Rolf Carlé.*

And of Clay Are We Created

Short Story by Isabel Allende

CLOSE READ
Notes

1. **READ ▶** As you read lines 1–30, begin to collect and cite evidence from the text.

- Circle the image that opens the story.
- In the margin, explain what the author foreshadows will happen to Carlé (lines 1–11).
- Underline text describing the consequences of the eruption.

They discovered the girl's head protruding from the mud pit, eyes wide open, calling soundlessly. She had a First Communion name, Azucena. Lily. In that vast cemetery where the odor of death was already attracting vultures from far away, and where the weeping of orphans and wails of the injured filled the air, the little girl obstinately clinging to life became the symbol of the tragedy. The television cameras transmitted so often the unbearable image of the head budding like a black squash from the clay that there was no one who did not recognize her and know her name. And every time we saw her on the screen, right behind her was Rolf Carlé, who had
10 gone there on assignment, never suspecting that he would find a fragment of his past, lost thirty years before.

First a **subterranean** sob rocked the cotton fields, curling them like waves of foam. Geologists had set up their seismographs weeks before and knew that the mountain had awakened again. For some time they had

subterranean:

predicted that the heat of the eruption could detach the eternal ice from the slopes of the volcano, but no one heeded their warnings; they sounded like the tales of frightened old women. The towns in the valley went about their daily life, deaf to the moaning of the earth, until that fateful Wednesday night in November when a prolonged roar announced the end of the world, 20 and walls of snow broke loose, rolling in an avalanche of clay, stones, and water that descended on the villages and buried them beneath unfathomable meters of telluric[1] vomit. As soon as the survivors emerged from the paralysis of that first awful terror, they could see that houses, plazas, churches, white cotton plantations, dark coffee forests, cattle pastures—all had disappeared. Much later, after soldiers and volunteers had arrived to rescue the living and try to assess the magnitude of the **cataclysm**, it was calculated that beneath the mud lay more than twenty thousand human beings and an indefinite number of animals putrefying in a viscous soup. Forests and rivers had also been swept away, and there was 30 nothing to be seen but an immense desert of mire.

When the station called before dawn, Rolf Carlé and I were together. I crawled out of bed, dazed with sleep, and went to prepare coffee while he hurriedly dressed. He stuffed his gear in the green canvas backpack he always carried, and we said goodbye, as we had so many times before. I had no **presentiments**. I sat in the kitchen, sipping my coffee and planning the long hours without him, sure that he would be back the next day.

He was one of the first to reach the scene, because while other reporters were fighting their way to the edges of that morass in jeeps, bicycles, or on foot, each getting there however he could, Rolf Carlé had the advantage of

cataclysm:

presentiment:

---

[1] **telluric:** of or relating to the earth.

2. **◄ REREAD** Reread lines 1–11. How does the narrator describe Carlé? Make an inference about his character based on this and the description of the devastation in lines 20–30. Cite text evidence in your response.

_____

_____

_____

_____

3. **READ ▷** As you read lines 31–65, continue to cite textual evidence.

• Underline text that describes Carlé's job.
• Circle the narrator's comments about how using a camera affects Carlé.

Armero, Colombia after the eruption of the Nevado del Ruiz volcano.

40 the television helicopter, which flew him over the avalanche. We watched on our screens the footage captured by his assistant's camera, in which he was up to his knees in muck, a microphone in his hand, in the midst of a bedlam of lost children, wounded survivors, corpses, and devastation. The story came to us in his calm voice. For years he had been a familiar figure in newscasts, reporting live at the scene of battles and catastrophes with awesome tenacity. Nothing could stop him, and I was always amazed at his **equanimity** in the face of danger and suffering; it seemed as if nothing could shake his fortitude or deter his curiosity. Fear seemed never to touch him, although he had confessed to me that he was not a courageous man,

50 far from it. I believe that the lens of a camera had a strange effect on him; it was as if it transported him to a different time from which he could watch events without actually participating in them. When I knew him better, I came to realize that this **fictive** distance seemed to protect him from his own emotions.

equanimity:

fictive:

4. ◀ **REREAD** Reread lines 31–54. Summarize what you know about the narrator and her relationship with Carlé. What can you infer about their emotional connection? Support your answer with textual evidence.

_____

_____

_____

_____

_____

_____

Rolf Carlé was in on the story of Azucena from the beginning. He filmed the volunteers who discovered her, and the first persons who tried to reach her; his camera zoomed in on the girl, her dark face, her large desolate eyes, the plastered-down tangle of her hair. The mud was like quicksand around her, and anyone attempting to reach her was in danger of sinking.

60 They threw a rope to her that she made no effort to grasp until they shouted to her to catch it; then she pulled a hand from the mire and tried to move but immediately sank a little deeper. Rolf threw down his knapsack and the rest of his equipment and waded into the quagmire, commenting for his assistant's microphone that it was cold and that one could begin to smell the stench of corpses.

"What's your name?" he asked the girl, and she told him her flower name. "Don't move, Azucena," Rolf Carlé directed, and kept talking to her, without a thought for what he was saying, just to distract her, while slowly he worked his way forward in mud up to his waist. The air around him

70 seemed as murky as the mud.

It was impossible to reach her from the approach he was attempting, so he retreated and circled around where there seemed to be firmer footing. When finally he was close enough, he took the rope and tied it beneath her arms, so they could pull her out. He smiled at her with that smile that crinkles his eyes and makes him look like a little boy; he told her that everything was fine, that he was here with her now, that soon they would have her out. He signaled the others to pull, but as soon as the cord tensed, the girl screamed. They tried again, and her shoulders and arms appeared, but they could move her no farther; she was trapped. Someone suggested

80 that her legs might be caught in the collapsed walls of her house, but she said it was not just rubble, that she was also held by the bodies of her brothers and sisters clinging to her legs.

5. **READ** ▶ As you read lines 66–129, continue to cite textual evidence.

- Underline the actions Carlé undertakes to help Azucena.
- Circle text describing Carlé's attempt to get the pump and what he envisions will happen once it arrives.
- In the margin, make an inference about how Carlé feels as he tries to rescue Azucena (lines 71–82).

"Don't worry, we'll get you out of here," Rolf promised. Despite the quality of the transmission, I could hear his voice break, and I loved him more than ever. Azucena looked at him but said nothing.

During those first hours Rolf Carlé exhausted all the resources of his **ingenuity** to rescue her. He struggled with poles and ropes, but every tug was an intolerable torture for the imprisoned girl. It occurred to him to use one of the poles as a lever but got no result and had to abandon the idea. He
90   talked a couple of soldiers into working with him for a while, but they had to leave because so many other victims were calling for help. The girl could not move, she barely could breathe, but she did not seem desperate, as if an ancestral resignation allowed her to accept her fate. The reporter, on the other hand, was determined to snatch her from death. Someone brought him a tire, which he placed beneath her arms like a life buoy, and then laid a plank near the hole to hold his weight and allow him to stay closer to her. As it was impossible to remove the rubble blindly, he tried once or twice to dive toward her feet but emerged frustrated, covered with mud, and spitting gravel. He concluded that he would have to have a pump to drain the water,
100   and radioed a request for one but received in return a message that there was no available transport and it could not be sent until the next morning.

"We can't wait that long!" Rolf Carlé shouted, but in the pandemonium no one stopped to **commiserate**. Many more hours would go by before he accepted that time had stagnated and reality had been irreparably distorted.

A military doctor came to examine the girl and observed that her heart was functioning well and that if she did not get too cold she could survive the night.

"Hang on, Azucena, we'll have the pump tomorrow," Rolf Carlé tried to console her.

110   "Don't leave me alone," she begged.

"No, of course I won't leave you."

Someone brought him coffee, and he helped the girl drink it, sip by sip. The warm liquid revived her, and she began telling him about her small life, about her family and her school, about how things were in that little bit of world before the volcano erupted. She was thirteen, and she had never been outside her village. Rolf Carlé, buoyed by a premature optimism, was convinced that everything would end well: the pump would arrive, they would drain the water, move the rubble, and Azucena would be transported by helicopter to a hospital where she would recover rapidly and where he
120   could visit her and bring her gifts. He thought, She's already too old for dolls, and I don't know what would please her; maybe a dress. I don't know

ingenuity:

commiserate:

© Houghton Mifflin Harcourt Publishing Company

much about women, he concluded, amused, reflecting that although he had known many women in his lifetime, none had taught him these details. To pass the hours he began to tell Azucena about his travels and adventures as a news hound, and when he exhausted his memory, he called upon imagination, inventing things he thought might entertain her. From time to time she dozed, but he kept talking in the darkness, to assure her that he was still there and to overcome the menace of uncertainty.

That was a long night.

130   Many miles away, I watched Rolf Carlé and the girl on a television screen. I could not bear the wait at home, so I went to National Television, where I often spent entire nights with Rolf editing programs. There, I was near his world, and I could at least get a feeling of what he lived through during those three decisive days. I called all the important people in the city, senators, commanders of the armed forces, the North American ambassador, and the president of National Petroleum, begging them for a pump to remove the silt, but obtained only vague promises. I began to ask for urgent help on radio and television, to see if there wasn't *someone* who could help us. Between calls I would run to the newsroom to monitor the

140   satellite transmissions that periodically brought new details of the catastrophe. While reporters selected scenes with most impact for the news report, I searched for footage that featured Azucena's mud pit. The screen reduced the disaster to a single plane and accentuated the tremendous distance that separated me from Rolf Carlé; nonetheless, I was there with

---

6. ◀ **REREAD** Reread lines 86–129. What do you learn about Rolf and Azucena in these lines? What do the last two sentences suggest about Rolf's character?

_____

_____

_____

_____

7. **READ** ▶ As you read lines 130–207, continue to cite textual evidence.

• Underline text explaining how the narrator tries to feel close to Carlé.

• Circle text describing how Carlé tried to help Azucena.

• In the margin, explain what the narrator means when she says Carlé "had completely forgotten the camera" (lines 174–175).

> # " The child's every suffering hurt me as it did him; I felt his frustration, his impotence. "

him. The child's every suffering hurt me as it did him; I felt his frustration, his impotence. Faced with the impossibility of communicating with him, the fantastic idea came to me that if I tried, I could reach him by force of mind and in that way give him encouragement. I concentrated until I was dizzy—a frenzied and futile activity. At times I would be overcome with 150 compassion and burst out crying; at other times, I was so drained I felt as if I were staring through a telescope at the light of a star dead for a million years.

I watched that hell on the first morning broadcast, cadavers of people and animals awash in the current of new rivers formed overnight from the melted snow. Above the mud rose the tops of trees and the bell towers of a church where several people had taken refuge and were patiently awaiting rescue teams. Hundreds of soldiers and volunteers from the civil defense were clawing through rubble searching for survivors, while long rows of ragged specters awaited their turn for a cup of hot broth. Radio networks 160 announced that their phones were jammed with calls from families offering shelter to orphaned children. Drinking water was in scarce supply, along with gasoline and food. Doctors, resigned to amputating arms and legs without anesthesia, pled that at least they be sent serum and painkillers and antibiotics; most of the roads, however, were impassable, and worse were the **bureaucratic** obstacles that stood in the way. To top it all, the clay contaminated by decomposing bodies threatened the living with an outbreak of epidemics.

bureaucratic:

Azucena was shivering inside the tire that held her above the surface. Immobility and tension had greatly weakened her, but she was conscious 170 and could still be heard when a microphone was held out to her. Her tone was humble, as if apologizing for all the fuss. Rolf Carlé had a growth of beard, and dark circles beneath his eyes; he looked near exhaustion. Even from that enormous distance I could sense the quality of his weariness, so different from the fatigue of other adventures. He had completely forgotten

CLOSE READ
Notes

The search for victims and survivors continues in Guayabal, Colombia after the eruption of the Nevado del Ruiz volcano (November 16, 1985).

the camera; he could not look at the girl through a lens any longer. The pictures we were receiving were not his assistant's but those of other reporters who had appropriated Azucena, bestowing on her the pathetic responsibility of embodying the horror of what had happened in that place. With the first light Rolf tried again to dislodge the obstacles that held the girl in her tomb, but he had only his hands to work with; he did not dare use a tool for fear of injuring her. He fed Azucena a cup of the cornmeal mush and bananas the army was distributing, but she immediately vomited it up. A doctor stated that she had a fever but added that there was little he could do: antibiotics were being reserved for cases of gangrene. A priest also passed by and blessed her, hanging a medal of the Virgin around her neck. By evening a gentle, persistent drizzle began to fall.

"The sky is weeping," Azucena murmured, and she, too, began to cry.

"Don't be afraid," Rolf begged. "You have to keep your strength up and be calm. Everything will be fine. I'm with you, and I'll get you out somehow."

Reporters returned to photograph Azucena and ask her the same questions, which she no longer tried to answer. In the meanwhile, more television and movie teams arrived with spools of cable, tapes, film, videos, precision lenses, recorders, sound consoles, lights, reflecting screens,

180

190

auxiliary motors, cartons of supplies, electricians, sound technicians, and cameramen: Azucena's face was beamed to millions of screens around the world. And all the while Rolf Carlé kept pleading for a pump. The improved technical facilities bore results, and National Television began receiving sharper pictures and clearer sound, the distance seemed suddenly

200   compressed, and I had the horrible sensation that Azucena and Rolf were by my side, separated from me by impenetrable glass. I was able to follow events hour by hour; I knew everything my love did to wrest the girl from her prison and help her endure her suffering; I overheard fragments of what they said to one another and could guess the rest; I was present when she taught Rolf to pray and when he distracted her with the stories I had told him in a thousand and one nights beneath the white mosquito netting of our bed.

   When darkness came on the second day, Rolf tried to sing Azucena to sleep with old Austrian folk songs he had learned from his mother, but she

210   was far beyond sleep. They spent most of the night talking, each in a stupor of exhaustion and hunger and shaking with cold. That night, imperceptibly, the unyielding floodgates that had contained Rolf Carlé's past for so many years began to open, and the torrent of all that had lain hidden in the deepest and most secret layers of memory poured out, leveling before it the obstacles that had blocked his consciousness for so long. He could not tell it all to Azucena; she perhaps did not know there was a world beyond the sea or time previous to her own; she was not capable of imagining Europe in

8. **◀ REREAD** Reread lines 191–207. In the margin, explain what the narrator says about television and intimacy. In what way is it ironic that the improved transmission equipment makes it to the scene while the pump remains unobtainable?

_____

_____

_____

_____

9. **READ ▶** As you read lines 208–268, continue to cite textual evidence.

- In the margin, explain what you learn about Carlé's past (lines 217–224 and lines 232–248).
- Circle text explaining why Carlé feels he must confront his own fears.
- Underline what Rolf learns about why he takes risks.

the years of the war. So he could not tell her of defeat, nor of the afternoon
the Russians had led them to the concentration camp to bury prisoners
220 dead from starvation. Why should he describe to her how the naked bodies
piled like a mountain of firewood resembled fragile china? How could he
tell this dying child about ovens and gallows? Nor did he mention the night
that he had seen his mother naked, shod in stiletto-heeled red boots,
sobbing with humiliation. There was much he did not tell, but in those
hours he relived for the first time all the things his mind had tried to erase.
Azucena had surrendered her fear to him and so, without wishing it, had
obliged Rolf to confront his own. There, beside that hellhole of mud, it was
impossible for Rolf to flee from himself any longer, and the **visceral** terror
he had lived as a boy suddenly invaded him. He reverted to the years when
230 he was the age of Azucena and younger, and, like her, found himself trapped
in a pit without escape, buried in life, his head barely above ground; he saw
before his eyes the boots and legs of his father, who had removed his belt
and was whipping it in the air with the never-forgotten hiss of a viper coiled
to strike. Sorrow flooded through him, intact and precise, as if it had lain
always in his mind, waiting. He was once again in the armoire where his
father locked him to punish him for imagined misbehavior, there where for
eternal hours he had crouched with his eyes closed, not to see the darkness,
with his hands over his ears to shut out the beating of his heart, trembling,
huddled like a cornered animal. Wandering in the mist of his memories he
240 found his sister, Katharina, a sweet, retarded child who spent her life
hiding, with the hope that her father would forget the disgrace of her having
been born. With Katharina, Rolf crawled beneath the dining room table,
and with her hid there under the long white tablecloth, two children forever
embraced, alert to footsteps and voices. Katharina's scent melded with his
own sweat, with aromas of cooking, garlic, soup, freshly baked bread, and
the unexpected odor of putrescent clay. His sister's hand in his, her
frightened breathing, her silk hair against his cheek, the candid gaze of her
eyes. Katharina . . . Katharina materialized before him, floating on the air
like a flag, clothed in the white tablecloth, now a winding sheet, and at last
250 he could weep for her death and for the guilt of having abandoned her. He
understood then that all his exploits as a reporter, the feats that had won
him such recognition and fame, were merely an attempt to keep his most
ancient fears at bay, a stratagem for taking refuge behind a lens to test
whether reality was more tolerable from that perspective. He took excessive
risks as an exercise of courage, training by day to conquer the monsters that
tormented him by night. But he had to come face to face with the moment
of truth; he could not continue to escape his past. He was Azucena; he was
buried in the clayey mud; his terror was not the distant emotion of an
almost forgotten childhood, it was a claw sunk in his throat. In the flush of

visceral:

260 his tears he saw his mother, dressed in black and clutching her imitation-crocodile pocketbook to her bosom, just as he had last seen her on the dock when she had come to put him on the boat to South America. She had not come to dry his tears, but to tell him to pick up a shovel: the war was over and now they must bury the dead.

"Don't cry. I don't hurt anymore. I'm fine," Azucena said when dawn came.

"I'm not crying for you," Rolf Carlé smiled. "I'm crying for myself. I hurt all over."

270 The third day in the valley of the cataclysm began with a pale light filtering through storm clouds. The president of the republic visited the area in his tailored safari jacket to confirm that this was the worst catastrophe of the century; the country was in mourning; sister nations had offered aid; he had ordered a state of siege; the armed forces would be merciless; anyone caught stealing or committing other offenses would be shot on sight. He added that it was impossible to remove all the corpses or count the thousands who had disappeared; the entire valley would be declared holy ground, and bishops would come to celebrate a solemn mass for the souls of the victims. He went to the army field tents to offer relief in the form of vague promises to crowds of the rescued, then to the improvised hospital to

---

10. **◀ REREAD** Reread lines 208–268. In what way is Carlé's interaction with Azucena changing him?

_____

_____

_____

_____

_____

_____

11. **READ ▶** As you read lines 269–310, continue to cite textual evidence.

- Circle adjectives the narrator uses that indicate her feelings about the president and his actions.

- Underline text that describes the interactions between Carlé and Azucena.

The town of Armero, Colombia, submerged by floods after the Nevado del Ruiz volcano erupted (November, 18, 1985).

offer a word of encouragement to doctors and nurses worn down from so many hours of tribulations. Then he asked to be taken to see Azucena, the little girl the whole world had seen. He waved to her with a limp statesman's hand, and microphones recorded his emotional voice and paternal tone as he told her that her courage had served as an example to the nation. Rolf Carlé interrupted to ask for a pump, and the president assured him that he personally would attend to the matter. I caught a glimpse of Rolf for a few seconds kneeling beside the mud pit. On the evening news broadcast, he was still in the same position; and I, glued to the screen like a fortune teller to her crystal ball, could tell that something fundamental had changed in him. I knew somehow that during the night his defenses had crumbled and he had given in to grief; finally he was vulnerable. The girl had touched a part of him that he himself had no access to, a part he had never shared with me. Rolf had wanted to console her, but it was Azucena who had given him consolation.

I recognized the precise moment at which Rolf gave up the fight and surrendered to the torture of watching the girl die. I was with them, three days and two nights, spying on them from the other side of life. I was there when she told him that in all her thirteen years no boy had ever loved her and that it was a pity to leave this world without knowing love. Rolf assured

280

290

12. **◀ REREAD** Reread lines 269–286. In the margin, make an inference about how the narrator feels about the president's visit. Support your answer with explicit textual evidence.

300 her that he loved her more than he could ever love anyone, more than he
loved his mother, more than his sister, more than all the women who had
slept in his arms, more than he loved me, his life companion, who would
have given anything to be trapped in that well in her place, who would have
exchanged her life for Azucena's, and I watched as he leaned down to kiss
her poor forehead, consumed by a sweet, sad emotion he could not name. I
felt how in that instant both were saved from despair, how they were freed
from the clay, how they rose above the vultures and helicopters, how
together they flew above the vast swamp of corruption and laments. How,
finally, they were able to accept death. Rolf Carlé prayed in silence that she
310 would die quickly, because such pain cannot be borne.

By then I had obtained a pump and was in touch with a general who
had agreed to ship it the next morning on a military cargo plane. But on the
night of that third day, beneath the unblinking focus of quartz lamps and
the lens of a hundred cameras, Azucena gave up, her eyes locked with those
of the friend who had sustained her to the end. Rolf Carlé removed the life
buoy, closed her eyelids, held her to his chest for a few moments, and then
let her go. She sank slowly, a flower in the mud.

You are back with me, but you are not the same man. I often
accompany you to the station, and we watch the videos of Azucena again;

13. **READ** ▶ As you read lines 311–326, continue to cite textual evidence.

• Underline text that describes what happens between Carlé and Azucena.
• Circle text describing how Carlé is no longer the person he used to be.

320 you study them intently, looking for something you could have done to save
her, something you did not think of in time. Or maybe you study them to
see yourself as if in a mirror, naked. Your cameras lie forgotten in a closet;
you do not write or sing; you sit long hours before the window, staring at
the mountains. Beside you, I wait for you to complete the voyage into
yourself, for the old wounds to heal. I know that when you return from your
nightmares, we shall again walk hand in hand, as before.

14. ◀ **REREAD AND DISCUSS** Reread lines 318–326. With a small group,
discuss the author's switch to second person point of view in these lines.
Why does she do this, and what effect does it have on you as a reader?

SHORT RESPONSE

Cite Text Evidence What is a theme of the story? Review your reading
notes and **cite text evidence** to support your answer.

_____

_____

_____

_____

_____

_____

_____

_____

_____

_____

_____

_____

_____

Background *One of the world's most accomplished adults with autism,* **Temple Grandin** *is a professor at Colorado State University. She is also the author of several best-selling books, including* Animals In Translation *from which this excerpt is taken. Drawing upon her long career as an animal scientist and her own experiences with autism,* Animals in Translation *provides a unique message about the way animals act, think, and feel.* **Catherine Johnson,** *Grandin's coauthor, specializes in writing about the brain. She is also no stranger to autism—two of her sons are autistic.*

from
Animals in Translation

Science Writing by Temple Grandin and Catherine Johnson

1. **READABLE** As you read lines 1–8, begin to collect and cite text evidence.

   • Underline the claim Grandin makes about animal perception in the first paragraph, and restate it in the margin.
   • Circle the sentence that explains what most people think about animals.
   • Underline Grandin's claim in the second paragraph.

CLOSE READ
Notes

Extreme Perception: The Mystery of Jane's Cat

Compared to humans, animals have astonishing abilities to perceive things in the world. They have *extreme perception*. Their sensory[1] worlds are so much richer than ours it's almost as if we're deaf and blind.

That's probably why a lot of people think animals have ESP.[2] Animals have such incredible abilities to perceive things we can't that the only explanation we can come up with is extrasensory perception. There's even a scientist in England who's written books about animals having ESP. But they don't have ESP, they just have a supersensitive sensory apparatus.

---

[1] **sensory:** of or related to any of the five senses.
[2] **ESP:** an abbreviation for extrasensory perception, the act of perceiving or communicating by means other than the five senses.

10   Take the cat who knows when its owner is coming home. My friend Jane, who lives in a city apartment, has a cat who always knows when she's on her way home. Jane's husband works at home, and five minutes before Jane comes home he'll see the cat go to the door, sit down, and wait. Since Jane doesn't come home at the same time every day, the cat isn't going by its sense of time, although animals also have an incredible sense of time. Sigmund Freud[3] used to have his dog with him every time he saw a patient, and he never had to look at his watch to tell when the session was over. The dog always let him know. Parents tell me autistic kids do the same thing. The only explanation Jane and her husband could come up with was ESP. The cat must have been picking up Jane's I'm-coming-home-now thoughts.

20   Jane asked me to figure out how her cat could predict her arrival. Since I've never seen Jane's apartment I used my mother's New York City apartment as a model for solving the mystery. In my imagination I watched my mother's gray Persian cat walk around the apartment and look out the

---

[3] **Sigmund Freud:** Austrian founder of psychoanalysis whose theories significantly influenced modern thought.

2. ◀ **REREAD** Reread lines 1–8. In your own words, explain the claim that Grandin makes about animals and ESP. What analogy does she make to get across her point about animals' "abilities to perceive the world"? Support your answer with explicit textual evidence.

_____

_____

_____

_____

_____

_____

3. **READ ▶** As you read lines 9–28, continue to cite textual evidence.

- Underline text describing the perceptive behavior of Jane's cat.
- Restate the claim that Jane and her husband make about her cat in the margin (lines 9–19).
- Circle the claim that Grandin gives to account for the cat's behavior, and restate it in the margin (lines 24–28).

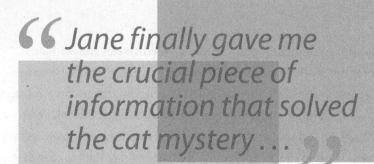

> *Jane finally gave me the crucial piece of information that solved the cat mystery . . .*

window. Possibly the cat could see Jane walking down the street. Even though he would not be able to see Jane's face from the twelfth floor he would probably be able to recognize her body language. Animals are very sensitive to body language. The cat would probably be able to recognize Jane's walk.

Next I thought about sound cues. Since I am a visual thinker I used "videos" in my imagination to move the cat around in the apartment to determine how it could be getting sound cues that Jane would be arriving a few minutes later. In my mind's eye I positioned the cat with its ear next to the crack between the door and the door frame. I thought maybe he could hear Jane's voice on the elevator. But as I played a tape of my mother getting onto the elevator in the lobby, I realized that there would be many days when Mother would ride the elevator alone and silent. She would speak on the elevator for only some of the trips—when there were other people in the elevator car with her—but not all of them.

So I asked Jane, "Is the cat always at the door, or is he at the door only sometimes?"

She said the cat is always at the door.

That meant the cat had to be hearing Jane's voice on the elevator every day. After I questioned her some more, Jane finally gave me the crucial piece of information that solved the cat mystery: her building does not have a push-button elevator. The elevator is operated by a person. So when Jane got on the elevator she probably said "Hi" to the operator.

---

4. ◀ **REREAD AND DISCUSS** With a small group, discuss whether you believe Grandin's explanation for the cat's behavior in lines 24–28. Why or why not?

5. **READ** ▶ As you read lines 29–58, underline places in the text where Grandin refers to her experiences with autism.

A new image flashed into my head. I created an elevator with an operator for my mother's building. To make the image I used the same method people use in computer graphics. I pulled an image of my mother's
50   elevator out of memory and combined it with an image of the elevator operator I saw one time at the Ritz in Boston. He had white gloves and a black tuxedo. I lifted the brass elevator control panel and its tuxedoed operator from my Ritz memory file and placed them inside my mother's elevator.

That was the answer. The fact that Jane's building had an elevator operator provided the cat with the sound of Jane's voice while Jane was still down on the first floor. That's why the cat went to the door to wait. The cat wasn't predicting Jane's arrival; for the cat Jane was already home.

6.   **◀ REREAD** As you reread lines 29–54, note in the margin how Grandin's experiences with autism led her to solve the mystery of Jane's cat.

SHORT RESPONSE

Cite Text Evidence Did Grandin's story about Jane's cat convince you that animals have an amazing ability to perceive their world. Why or why not? Explain, **citing evidence from the text** in your response.

_____

_____

_____

_____

_____

_____

_____

_____

_____

_____

Background *Poems about family often give us insights not only into the author's life and upbringing, but also into our own. As you read the two poems selected here, think of these lines written by the poet Dylan Thomas: "You can tear a poem apart to see what makes it tick . . . You're back with the mystery of having been moved by words. The best craftsmanship always leaves holes and gaps . . . so that something that is not in the poem can creep, crawl, flash or thunder in."*

Poems About Family

My Ceremony For Taking . . . . Lara Mann
The Stayer . . . . Virgil Suárez

Lara Mann *was born in Kansas, and is a member of the Choctaw Nation of Oklahoma. She is of English, Irish, Choctaw, French, German, Scottish, Spanish, Cherokee, Welsh, and Mohawk descent. Common themes in her work include the integration of both Native American and American culture and exposing the inaccurate stereotypes that many Americans assign to Native Americans.*

Virgil Suárez *By the time Virgil Suárez was twelve years old, his family had moved across the ocean twice—first from Cuba to Spain and then from Spain to the United States. These childhood experiences continue to influence the predominant themes of Suárez's works— family ties, immigration, and exile. He draws upon his own memories of people and places for his work, and credits his family for providing him with such an interesting array of characters. He notes, "I write about my life, and my life informs my writing."*

1. **READ ▶** As you read lines 1–24, begin to collect and cite text evidence.

   • Underline words and phrases that have similar meanings.
   • Circle examples of figurative language.
   • In the margin, write your interpretation of lines 1–5.

My Ceremony For Taking
Lara Mann

No one told me how it should be, these steps
for taking. Some things I know without being told.
The words told to me ended my family,
the words I told burned my family's death scaffold;
those things we say when we are hurt, to hurt.   5

I wanted to take pieces of my ancestor's
homes with me, the way some homelands are sacred.
The way some carry their birth dirt for protection.
But these locations are revered, and for me,
the taking was blasphemous.   10

My parents split, and I felt
absolutely halved, though what was left of me
was unclear. I needed a ceremony.
It had to require pain,
a sacrifice. It had to be missed.   15

That summer, when we went, my dad and I,
back to Alabama and Mississippi
to try to fix our **fissured** selves.
I pulled out hair many times.

Choctaws were known for hair: long, thick, honor-   20
banner. I gave of myself. My hair was my thanks:
parts of me pulled out, white-root waving; a lock,
not just a strand, pressed into the dirt I took
for payment, to leave part of myself.

fissure:

2. **◀ REREAD** Reread lines 11–24 of "My Ceremony For Taking." In the margin, explain why the speaker feels "split."

3. **READ ▶** As you read lines 1–34 of "The Stayer," collect and cite text evidence.

- Circle reasons for Chicho staying in Cuba.
- In the margin, explain why Chicho is called "crazy."
- Underline figurative language, or descriptive words, that create tone.

The Stayer
Virgil Suárez

Simply, my uncle Chicho stayed
   back in Cuba, against the family's
advice, because everyone left

   and he chose to stay, and this act
5 of staying marked him as "crazy"
   with most of the men, and he stayed

   there in a shack behind my aunt's
   clapboard house, sat in the dark
of most days in the middle

10 of the packed-dirt floor and nodded
at the insistence of light, the way
   it darted through holes in the tin

   roof where the rain drummed
   like the gallop of spooked horses.
15 This is where he was born, he chanted

   under his breath to no one, why should
he leave, live in perpetual longing
   within exile? He learned long ago

to count the passing of time
20   in how **motes** danced in the shaft
of white light, the *chicharras*[1] echoed

   their trill against the emptiness
of life, against the wake of resistance
   in this place he knew as a child,

motes:

---

[1] ***chicharras:*** cicadas, insects that produce a loud buzzing noise.

25   as a man, *un hombre*, bend against the idea
         of leaving his country, call him loco.[2]
      What nobody counted on was that answers

         come on to those who sit in the
      quiet of their own countries, tranquil

penumbra: 30   in the **penumbra**, intent on hearing the song

         of a *tomegüín*[3] as it calls for a mate
            to come nest in the shrubs out there,
      while in here, he witnesses how light

         fills the emptiness with the meaning of stay.

      ---

      [2] *loco*: crazy.
      [3] *tomegüín*: a small bird native to Cuba.

---

4. ◀ **REREAD** Reread "The Stayer." How does the phrase "live in perpetual
longing within exile" reflect the overall meaning of the poem?

_____

_____

_____

SHORT RESPONSE

Cite Text Evidence   In what ways does each poet use figurative language to
communicate a large or complex idea? **Cite evidence from the text.**

_____

_____

_____

_____

_____

_____

_____

_____

Sweet Sorrow

Sweet Sorrow

"Love is the great intangible."

—Diane Ackerman

DRAMA

from The Tragedy of
Romeo and Juliet
  Prologue
  Act II. Scene 2

William Shakespeare

Background *It sounds like a love story ripped from the tabloids. Two teenagers fall in love. Then they learn that their parents hate one another. Murder and suffering follow, and by the end, a whole town is mourning. What love can—and cannot—overcome is at the core of* Romeo and Juliet, *considered by many to be the greatest love story of all time. This play by* **William Shakespeare** *(1564–1616) was one of his earlier works. It was probably first performed in the mid-1590s, when he would have been about thirty years old. As was the custom at that time, Shakespeare based his play on a story that already existed.*

from The Tragedy of Romeo and Juliet

Drama by William Shakespeare

CLOSE READ
Notes

CHARACTERS

THE MONTAGUES
Romeo

THE CAPULETS
Juliet

Nurse

OTHER
Chorus

TIME. *The 14th century*
PLACE. *Verona and Mantua in northern Italy*

1. **READ ▶** As you read the Prologue, begin to cite text evidence.

   - Circle text that describes the similar backgrounds of Romeo and Juliet.
   - Underline clues that tell what will happen to the title characters.
   - In the margin, explain how Shakespeare sets out one of the play's major themes—the conflict between love and hate.

The Chorus is an individual actor who serves as a narrator. He enters from the back of the stage to introduce and explain the theme of the play. His job is to "hook" the audience's interest by telling them just enough to quiet them down and make them eager for more. In this prologue, the Chorus explains the age-old feud between two prominent families of the Italian city of Verona.

PROLOGUE

[*Enter* Chorus.]

Chorus. Two households, both alike in dignity,
In fair Verona, where we lay our scene,
From ancient grudge break to new **mutiny,**
Where civil blood makes civil hands unclean.
5   From forth the fatal loins of these two foes,
A pair of star-crossed[1] lovers take their life,[2]
Whose misadventured[3] piteous overthrows
Doth with their death bury their parents' strife.
The fearful passage of their death-marked love,
10   And the continuance of their parents' rage,
Which, but their children's end, naught could remove,
Is now the two hours' traffic of our stage,
The which if you with patient ears attend,
What here shall miss, our toil shall strive to mend.

[*Exit.*]

---

[1] **star-crossed:** doomed. The position of the stars when the lovers were born was not favorable. In Shakespeare's day, people took astrology very seriously.

[2] **take their life:** are born, begin their lives.

[3] **misadventured:** unlucky.

mutiny:

2. **◀ REREAD** Reread lines 6–10. What effect does the Chorus say that death will have on the remaining characters?

3. **READ ▷** As you read lines 1–25 of Act II, Scene 2, continue to cite text evidence.

- Underline a metaphor that Romeo uses to describe Juliet.
- In the margin, explain Romeo's conflicting motivations (lines 13–14).

Prior to this scene, Romeo, a Montague, and his friends snuck into a masquerade ball given by the Capulet family. There, Romeo and Juliet, who is a Capulet, fall in love at first sight. Only after they talk and kiss do they discover they have fallen in love with the enemy. After the ball, Romeo hides in Lord Capulet's orchard, hoping for a chance to see Juliet on her balcony.

Act II

Scene 2 • *Capulet's orchard.*

[*Enter* Romeo.]

Romeo. He jests at scars that never felt a wound.[1]

[*Enter* Juliet *above at a window.*]

But soft! What light through yonder window breaks?

It is the East, and Juliet is the sun!

Arise, fair sun, and kill the envious moon,

5 Who is already sick and pale with grief

That thou her maid art far more fair than she.

Be not her maid, since she is envious;

Her vestal livery is but sick and green,

And none but fools do wear it; cast it off.

10 It is my lady; O, it is my love!

O that she knew she were!

She speaks, yet she says nothing. What of that?

Her eye discourses; I will answer it.

I am too bold; 'tis not to me she speaks.

15 Two of the fairest stars in all the heaven,

Having some business, do entreat[2] her eyes

To twinkle in their spheres till they return.

What if her eyes were there, they in her head?

The brightness of her cheek would shame those stars

---

[1] **He jests at scars that never felt a wound:** Earlier, Romeo's friend Mercutio makes fun of love. Here, Romeo says he makes fun of it because he has never been wounded by it.

[2] **entreat:** beg, urge.

20 As daylight doth a lamp; her eyes in heaven
    Would through the airy region stream so bright
    That birds would sing and think it were not night.
    See how she leans her cheek upon her hand!
    O that I were a glove upon that hand,
25 That I might touch that cheek!

Juliet.   Ay me!

Romeo.   She speaks.
    O, speak again, bright angel! for thou art
    As glorious to this night, being o'er my head,
    As is a winged messenger of heaven
    Unto the white-upturned wond'ring eyes
30 Of mortals that fall back to gaze on him
    When he bestrides[3] the lazy-pacing clouds
    And sails upon the bosom of the air.

Juliet. O Romeo, Romeo! Wherefore[4] art thou Romeo?
    Deny thy father and refuse thy name!
35 Or, if thou wilt not, be but sworn my love,
    And I'll no longer be a Capulet.

Romeo [*aside*]. Shall I hear more, or shall I speak at this?

Juliet. 'Tis but thy name that is my enemy.
    Thou art thyself, though not[5] a Montague.
40 What's Montague? It is nor hand, nor foot,
    Nor arm, nor face, nor any other part
    Belonging to a man. O, be some other name!
    What's in a name? That which we call a rose
    By any other name would smell as sweet.

---

[3] **bestrides:** stands on.
[4] **wherefore:** why.
[5] **though not:** if you were not.

---

4. ◀ **REREAD AND DISCUSS** Reread lines 1–25 of Act II, Scene 2. In a
   small group, discuss how Romeo expresses his love for Juliet. To what
   does he compare her eyes?

5. **READ** ▷ As you read lines 26–53, continue to cite evidence.

   • In the margin, explain what Juliet wants from Romeo (lines 33–36).
   • Underline the first lines where one character knowingly addresses the
     other directly.
   • Circle the lines where Juliet realizes she has been overheard.

45   So Romeo would, were he not Romeo called,

Retain that dear perfection which he owes[6]

Without that title. Romeo, doff[7] thy name;

And for that name, which is no part of thee,

Take all myself.

Romeo.   I take thee at thy word.

50   Call me but love, and I'll be new baptized;

Henceforth[8] I never will be Romeo.

Juliet. What man art thou that, thus bescreened[9] in night,

So stumblest on my counsel?[10]

   Romeo.   By a name

I know not how to tell thee who I am.

55   My name, dear saint, is hateful to myself,

Because it is an enemy to thee.

Had I it written, I would tear the word.

Juliet. My ears have yet not drunk a hundred words

Of that tongue's utterance,[11] yet I know the sound.

60   Art thou not Romeo, and a Montague?

Romeo. Neither, fair saint, if either thee dislike.

Juliet. How camest thou hither, tell me, and wherefore?

The orchard walls are high and hard to climb,

And the place death, considering who thou art,

65   If any of my kinsmen find thee here.

---

[6] **owes:** owns, possesses.

[7] **doff:** get rid of.

[8] **henceforth:** from now on.

[9] **bescreened:** hidden.

[10]**counsel:** thoughts.

[11]**utterance:** speech.

6. **◄ REREAD** Reread lines 38–49. What is Juliet saying about names here?

_____

_____

_____

7. **READ ▷** As you read lines 54–79, continue to cite textual evidence.

• Underline the text where Juliet worries about what will happen if her family finds Romeo on Capulet property.

• In the margin, explain what would distress Romeo more than facing death (lines 75–78).

Romeo. With love's light wings did I o'erperch these walls;

For stony limits cannot hold love out,

And what love can do, that dares love attempt.

Therefore thy kinsmen are no let[12] to me.

70 **Juliet.** If they do see thee, they will murder thee.

Romeo. Alack, there lies more peril in thine eye

Than twenty of their swords! Look thou but sweet,

And I am proof against their enmity.

Juliet. I would not for the world they saw thee here.

75 **Romeo.** I have night's cloak to hide me from their sight;

And but thou love me, let them find me here.

My life were better ended by their hate

Than death prorogued,[13] wanting of thy love.

Juliet. By whose direction foundst thou out this place?

80 **Romeo.** By love, that first did prompt me to enquire.

He lent me counsel, and I lent him eyes.

I am no pilot, yet, wert thou as far

As that vast shore washed with the farthest sea,

I would adventure for such merchandise.

85 **Juliet.** Thou knowest the mask of night is on my face;

Else would a maiden blush bepaint my cheek

For that which thou hast heard me speak tonight.

---

[12]**let:** hindrance, obstacle.

[13]**prorogued:** postponed.

---

8. ◀ **REREAD** Reread lines 62–79. Juliet has not spoken directly to Romeo of her feelings for him. What might be holding her back? What clues do you have about her emotions from her words here and earlier in Scene 2?

_____

_____

_____

9. **READ** ▶ As you read lines 80–106, continue to cite textual evidence.

• In the margin, explain how Juliet feels about being overheard by Romeo (lines 85–89).

• Underline lines that show Juliet is worried that she will make a bad impression on Romeo by falling for him too easily.

> ❝ *O gentle Romeo, if thou dost love, pronounce it faithfully.* ❞

Fain[14] would I dwell on form—fain, fain deny
What I have spoke; but farewell compliment!
90   Dost thou love me? I know thou wilt say "Ay";
And I will take thy word. Yet, if thou swearst,
Thou mayst prove false. At lovers' perjuries,
They say Jove[15] laughs. O gentle Romeo,
If thou dost love, pronounce it faithfully.
95   Or if thou thinkst I am too quickly won,
I'll frown, and be perverse, and say thee nay,
So thou wilt woo; but else, not for the world.
In truth, fair Montague, I am too fond,
And therefore thou mayst think my 'havior light;
100 But trust me, gentleman, I'll prove more true
Than those that have more cunning to be strange.[16]
I should have been more strange, I must confess,
But that thou overheardst, ere I was ware,[17]
My true love's passion. Therefore pardon me,
105 And not impute this yielding to light love,
Which the dark night hath so discovered.

---

[14] **fain:** willingly.

[15] **Jove:** another name for the Roman god Jupiter, king of the gods.

[16] **strange:** aloof, cold.

[17] **ware:** aware.

10. ◀ **REREAD** Reread lines 85–106. Explain the shifts in emotions Juliet experiences in this soliloquy.

_____

_____

_____

Romeo. Lady, by yonder blessed moon I swear,

That tips with silver all these fruit-tree tops—

Juliet. O, swear not by the moon, the inconstant moon,

110 That monthly changes in her circled orb,

Lest that thy love prove likewise variable.

Romeo. What shall I swear by?

Juliet.   Do not swear at all;

Or if thou wilt, swear by thy gracious self,

Which is the god of my idolatry,

115 And I'll believe thee.

Romeo.   If my heart's dear love—

Juliet. Well, do not swear. Although I joy in thee,

I have no joy of this contract[18] tonight.

It is too rash, too unadvised, too sudden;

Too like the lightning, which doth cease to be

120 Ere one can say "It lightens." Sweet, good night!

This bud of love, by summer's ripening breath,

May prove a beauteous flow'r when next we meet.

Good night, good night! As sweet repose and rest

Come to thy heart as that within my breast!

125 **Romeo.** O, wilt thou leave me so unsatisfied?

Juliet. What satisfaction canst thou have tonight?

Romeo. The exchange of thy love's faithful vow for mine.

Juliet. I gave thee mine before thou didst request it;

And yet I would it were to give again.

130 **Romeo.** Wouldst thou withdraw it? For what purpose, love?

Juliet. But to be frank and give it thee again.

And yet I wish but for the thing I have.

My bounty is as boundless as the sea,

My love as deep; the more I give to thee,

135 The more I have, for both are infinite.

I hear some noise within. Dear love, adieu!

----

[18] **contract:** declaration of love.

11. (**READ**) As you read lines 107–141, continue to cite textual evidence.

- Underline the line in which Romeo states what he wants of Juliet.
- Circle each time a character "swears" or promises something.
- In the margin, explain what Juliet is feeling.

[Nurse *calls within.*]

Anon[19], good nurse! Sweet Montague, be true.

Stay but a little, I will come again.

[*Exit.*]

Romeo. O blessed, blessed night! I am afeard,

140   Being in night, all this is but a dream,

Too flattering-sweet to be substantial.

[*Re-enter* Juliet, *above.*]

Juliet. Three words, dear Romeo, and good night indeed.

If that thy bent of love be honorable,

Thy purpose marriage, send me word tomorrow,

145   By one that I'll procure to come to thee,

Where and what time thou wilt perform the rite;

And all my fortunes at thy foot I'll lay

And follow thee my lord throughout the world.

Nurse [*within*]. Madam!

150   **Juliet.** I come, anon.—But if thou meanst not well,

I do beseech thee—

Nurse [*within*].   Madam!

Juliet.   By-and-by I come.

—To cease thy suit and leave me to my grief.

Tomorrow will I send.

---

[19]**anon:** right away.

---

12. **◀ REREAD** Reread lines 136–138. What happens in these lines? What other character is introduced here?

_____

_____

_____

_____

13. **READ ▶** As you read lines 142–169, continue to cite textual evidence.

- Underline the lines in which Juliet tells Romeo what she wants him to do.

- In the margin, explain the plans the couple makes. What does the audience already know from the prologue?

Romeo.   So thrive my soul—

Juliet. A thousand times good night! [*Exit.*]

155 **Romeo.** A thousand times the worse, to want thy light!

Love goes toward love as schoolboys from their books;

But love from love, towards school with heavy looks.

[*Enter* Juliet *again, above.*]

Juliet. Hist![20] Romeo, hist! O for a falc'ner's voice

To lure this tassel-gentle[21] back again!

160 Bondage is hoarse and may not speak aloud,

Else would I tear the cave where Echo lies,

And make her airy tongue more hoarse than mine

With repetition of my Romeo's name.

Romeo!

165 **Romeo.** It is my soul that calls upon my name.

How silver-sweet sound lovers' tongues by night,

Like softest music to attending ears!

Juliet. Romeo!

Romeo.   My sweet?

Juliet.   What o'clock tomorrow

Shall I send to thee?

Romeo.   By the hour of nine.

---

[20]**hist:** listen.

[21]**a falc'ner's voice, to lure this tassel-gentle:** A falconer trains and cares for tame falcons
used for hunting; a tassel-gentle (or tiercel-gentle) is a variety of falcon.

14. **◄ REREAD** Reread lines 142–169. How does Shakespeare use Juliet's
leaving and returning to reveal more about Juliet's feelings?

_____

_____

_____

_____

_____

_____

170 **Juliet.** I will not fail. 'Tis twenty years till then.

I have forgot why I did call thee back.

Romeo. Let me stand here till thou remember it.

Juliet. I shall forget, to have thee still stand there,

Rememb'ring how I love thy company.

175 **Romeo.** And I'll still stay, to have thee still forget,

Forgetting any other home but this.

Juliet. 'Tis almost morning. I would have thee gone—

And yet no farther than a wanton's²² bird,

That lets it hop a little from her hand,

180 Like a poor prisoner in his twisted gyves,²³

And with a silk thread plucks it back again,

So loving-jealous of his liberty.

Romeo. I would I were thy bird.

Juliet.   Sweet, so would I.

Yet I should kill thee with much cherishing.

_____

²²**wanton:** spoiled young girl.

²³**twisted gyves:** shackles.

15. **READ ▷** As you read lines 170–190, continue to cite textual evidence.

- Underline the promises Romeo and Juliet make to each other.

- In the margin, explain in your own words the meaning of Juliet's words to Romeo (lines 177–182).

16. **◁ REREAD** Reread lines 177–186. Note some examples of contradictions—saying opposite things—that Juliet says here. What does this tell you about Juliet's motivations?

_____

_____

_____

_____

_____

_____

_____

185   Good night, good night! Parting is such sweet sorrow,

That I shall say good night till it be morrow.

[*Exit.*]

Romeo. Sleep dwell upon thine eyes, peace in thy breast!

Would I were sleep and peace, so sweet to rest!

Hence will I to my ghostly father's[24] cell,

190   His help to crave and my dear hap[25] to tell.

[*Exit.*]

———————

[24]**ghostly father:** priest, spiritual advisor.
[25]**dear hap:** good fortune.

SHORT RESPONSE

Cite Text Evidence   Compare the tone of the Prologue to that of Act II, Scene 2. How might knowing the statements in the Prologue color an audience's view of the later scene between Romeo and Juliet? **Cite examples from the text** of the Prologue and Act II, Scene 2 as evidence.

_____

_____

_____

_____

_____

_____

_____

_____

_____

_____

_____

_____

A Matter of Life or Death

A Matter of Life or Death

"To endure what is unendurable is true endurance."

—Japanese proverb

Background *In 1994, a mass genocide took place in the East African state of Rwanda when Hutus killed 800,000 men, women, and children over a period of 100 days. Although tensions existed between the Hutus and Tutsis (the two main ethnic groups in Rwanda) for hundreds of years, things came to a head on April 6, 1994, when a plane carrying the President of Rwanda, a Hutu, was shot down. Many perceived this as an attack by Tutsis, and the tensions between the two groups escalated into full-blown violence.* **Paul Rusesabagina** *lived through the genocide and wrote about the horrors in his memoir* An Ordinary Man *(from which this excerpt comes), which later became the film* Hotel Rwanda.

from
An Ordinary Man

Memoir by Paul Rusesabagina

1. **READ ▷** As you read lines 1–43, begin to cite text evidence.

- Underline the actions Rusesabagina took when the genocide broke out.
- In the margin, explain what Rusesabagina has trouble understanding (lines 4–24).
- Circle words and phrases that convey a tone of disgust and horror.

My name is Paul Rusesabagina. I am a hotel manager. In April 1994, when a wave of mass murder broke out in my country, I was able to hide 1,268 people inside the hotel where I worked.

When the militia and the Army came with orders to kill my guests, I took them into my office, treated them like friends, offered them beer and cognac, and then persuaded them to neglect their task that day. And when they came back, I poured more drinks and kept telling them they should leave in peace once again. It went on like this for seventy-six days. I was not particularly **eloquent** in these conversations. They were no different from
10   the words I would have used in saner times to order a shipment of pillowcases, for example, or tell the shuttle van driver to pick up a guest at the airport. I still don't understand why those men in the militias didn't just put a bullet in my head and execute every last person in the rooms upstairs but they didn't. None of the refugees in my hotel were killed. Nobody was beaten. Nobody was taken away and made to disappear. People were being hacked to death with machetes all over Rwanda, but that five-story building

eloquent:

prevailed:

became a refuge for anyone who could make it to our doors. The hotel could offer only an illusion of safety, but for whatever reason, the illusion **prevailed** and I survived to tell the story, along with those I sheltered. There

20 was nothing particularly heroic about it. My only pride in the matter is that I stayed at my post and continued to do my job as manager when all other aspects of decent life vanished. I kept the Hotel Mille Collines open, even as the nation descended into chaos and eight hundred thousand people were butchered by their friends, neighbors, and countrymen.

It happened because of racial hatred. Most of the people hiding in my hotel were Tutsis, descendants of what had once been the ruling class of Rwanda. The people who wanted to kill them were mostly Hutus, who were traditionally farmers. The usual stereotype is that Tutsis are tall and thin with delicate noses, and Hutus are short and stocky with wider noses, but

30 most people in Rwanda fit neither description. This divide is mostly artificial, a leftover from history, but people take it very seriously, and the two groups have been living uneasily alongside each other for more than five hundred years.

You might say the divide also lives inside me. I am the son of a Hutu farmer and his Tutsi wife. My family cared not the least bit about this when I was growing up, but since bloodlines are passed through the father in Rwanda, I am technically a Hutu. I married a Tutsi woman, whom I love with a fierce passion, and we had a child of mixed descent together. This type of blended family is typical in Rwanda, even with our long history of

40 racial prejudice. Very often we can't tell each other apart just by looking at one another. But the difference between Hutu and Tutsi means everything in Rwanda. In the late spring and early summer of 1994 it meant the difference between life and death.

2. ◀ **REREAD** Reread lines 25–43. How do Rusesabagina's words convey his feelings about the division between Hutus and Tutsis? What is his purpose in describing his family when explaining these differences? Support your answer with explicit textual evidence.

_____

_____

_____

_____

Between April 6, when the plane of President Juvenal Habyarimana was shot down with a missile, and July 4, when the Tutsi rebel army captured the capital of Kigali, approximately eight hundred thousand Rwandans were slaughtered. This is a number that cannot be grasped with the rational mind. It is like trying—all at once—to understand that the earth is surrounded by billions of balls of gas just like our sun across a vast
50 blackness. You cannot understand the magnitude. Just try! Eight hundred thousand lives snuffed out in one hundred days. That's eight thousand lives a day. More than five lives per *minute*. Each one of those lives was like a little world in itself. Some person who laughed and cried and ate and thought and felt and hurt just like any other person, just like you and me. A mother's child, every one irreplaceable.

And the way they died . . . I can't bear to think about it for long. Many went slowly from slash wounds, watching their own blood gather in pools in the dirt, perhaps looking at their own severed limbs, oftentimes with the screams of their parents or their children or their husbands in their cars.
60 Their bodies were cast aside like garbage, left to rot in the sun, shoveled into mass graves with bulldozers when it was all over. It was not the largest genocide in the history of the world, but it was the fastest and most efficient.

At the end, the best you can say is that my hotel saved about four hours' worth of people. Take four hours away from one hundred days and you have an idea of just how little I was able to accomplish against the grand design.

3. **READ ▷** As you read lines 44–73, continue to cite evidence.

• Underline words or phrases that convey Rusesabagina's tone.

• In the margin, describe the tone of each paragraph.

• Circle the resources Rusesabagina used to save the people hiding at the hotel.

4. **◄ REREAD** Reread lines 44–55. What is Rusesabagina's purpose in these lines?

_____

_____

_____

_____

What did I have to work with? I had a five-story building. I had a cooler full of drinks. I had a small stack of cash in the safe. And I had a working telephone and I had my tongue. It wasn't much. Anybody with a gun or a machete could have taken these things away from me quite easily. My disappearance—and that of my family—would have barely been noticed in the torrents of blood coursing through Rwanda in those months. Our bodies would have joined the thousands in the east-running rivers floating toward Lake Victoria, their skins turning white with water rot.

I wonder today what exactly it was that allowed me to stop the killing clock for four hours.

There were a few things in my favor, but they do not explain everything. I was a Hutu because my father was Hutu, and this gave me a certain amount of protection against immediate execution. But it was not only Tutsis who were slaughtered in the genocide; it was also the thousands of moderate Hutus who were suspected of sympathizing with or even helping the Tutsi "cockroaches." I was certainly one of these cockroach-lovers. Under the standards of mad extremism at work then I was a prime candidate for a beheading.

Another surface advantage: I had control of a luxury hotel, which was one of the few places during the genocide that had the image of being protected by soldiers. But the important word in that sentence is *image*. In the opening days of the slaughter, the United Nations had left four unarmed soldiers staying at the hotel as guests. This was a symbolic gesture. I was also able to bargain for the service of five Kigali policemen. But I knew these men were like a wall of tissue paper standing between us and a flash flood.

Yet another of my advantages was a very strange one. I knew many of the architects of the genocide and had been friendly with them. It was, in a way, part of my job. I was the general manager of a hotel called the Diplomates, but I was eventually asked to take charge of a sister property, the nearby Hotel Mille Collines, where most of the events described in this book took place. The Mille Collines was *the* place in Kigali where the power

5. **READ ▶** As you read lines 74–109, continue to cite textual evidence.

- Underline the advantages Rusesabagina had at the time of the genocide.
- In the margin, explain why the word "image" is important in line 85.
- Circle two instances in which Rusesabagina mentions being at risk.

> *I wonder today what exactly it was that allowed me to stop the killing clock for four hours.*

classes of Rwanda came to meet Western businessmen and dignitaries. Before the killing started I had shared drinks with most of these men, served them complimentary plates of lobster, lit their cigarettes. I knew the names of their wives and their children. I had stored up a large bank of favors. I cashed them all in—and then borrowed heavily—during the genocide. My preexisting friendship with General Augustin Bizimungu in particular helped save the Mille Collines from being raided many times over. But **alliances** always shift, particularly in the chaos of war, and I knew my supply of liquor and favors would run dry in some crucial quarters. Before the hundred days were over a squad of soldiers was dispatched to kill me. I survived only after a desperate half hour during which I called in even more favors.

All these things helped me during the genocide. But they don't explain everything.

Let me tell you what I think was the most important thing of all.

I will never forget walking out of my house the first day of the killings. There were people in the streets who I had known for seven years, neighbors of mine who had come over to our place for our regular Sunday cookouts. These people were wearing military uniforms that had been handed out by the militia. They were holding machetes and were trying to get inside the houses of those they knew to be Tutsi, those who had Tutsi relatives, or those who refused to go along with the murders.

alliance:

6. **◄ REREAD AND DISCUSS** Reread lines 76–109. In a small group, discuss what else might have helped Rusesabagina survive the genocide.

7. **READ ▶** As you read lines 110–145, continue to cite textual evidence.

   • In the margin, explain why Rusesabagina included the story about Peter.
   • Underline text describing the "words" people had heard causing them to go "mad."

120　　There was one man in particular whom I will call Peter, though that is not his real name. He was a truck driver, about thirty years old, with a young wife. The best word I can use to describe him is an American word: *cool*. Peter was just a cool guy; so nice to children, very gentle, kind of a kidder, but never mean with his humor. I saw him that morning wearing a military uniform and holding a machete dripping in blood. Watching this happen in my own neighborhood was like looking up at a blue summer sky and seeing it suddenly turning to purple. The entire world had gone mad around me.

　　What had caused this to happen? Very simple: words.

130　　The parents of these people had been told over and over again that they were uglier and stupider than the Tutsis. They were told they would never be as physically attractive or as capable of running the affairs of the country. It was a poisonous stream of rhetoric designed to reinforce the power of the elite. When the Hutus came to power they spoke evil words of their own, fanning the old resentments, exciting the hysterical dark places in the heart.

exhortation:

　　The words put out by radio station announcers were a major cause of the violence. There were explicit **exhortations** for ordinary citizens to break into the homes of their neighbors and kill them where they stood. Those
140　　commands that weren't direct were phrased in code language that everybody understood: "Cut the tall trees. Clean your neighborhood. Do your duty." The names and addresses of targets were read over the air. If a person was able to run away his position and direction of travel were broadcast and the crowd followed the chase over the radio like a sports event.

8. **◀ REREAD** Reread lines 137–145. How does calling the hunt for Tutsis a "sports event" convey the tone of the narrative?

_____

_____

_____

_____

_____

_____

> *Words . . . can also be powerful tools of life.*

The avalanche of words celebrating racial supremacy and encouraging people to do their duty created an alternate reality in Rwanda for those three months. It was an atmosphere where the insane was made to seem normal and disagreement with the mob was fatal.

150   Rwanda was a failure on so many levels. It started as a failure of the European colonists who exploited trivial differences for the sake of a divide-and-rule strategy. It was the failure of Africa to get beyond its ethnic divisions and form true coalition governments. It was a failure of Western democracies to step in and avert the catastrophe when abundant evidence was available. It was a failure of the United States for not calling a genocide by its right name. It was the failure of the United Nations to live up to its commitments as a peacemaking body.

    All of these come down to a failure of words. And this is what I want to tell you: Words are the most effective weapons of death in man's **arsenal.**
160 But they can also be powerful tools of life. They may be the only ones.

    Today I am convinced that the only thing that saved those 1,268 people in my hotel was words. Not the liquor, not money, not the UN. Just ordinary words directed against the darkness. They are so important. I used words in many ways during the genocide—to plead, intimidate, coax, cajole, and negotiate. I was slippery and evasive when I needed to be. I acted friendly toward despicable people. I put cartons of champagne into their car trunks. I flattered them shamelessly. I said whatever I thought it would take to keep the people in my hotel from being killed. I had no cause to advance, no ideology to promote beyond that one simple goal. Those words were my
170 connection to a saner world, to life as it ought to be lived.

    I am not a politician or a poet. I built my career on words that are plain and ordinary and concerned with everyday details. I am nothing more or

arsenal:

---

9. **READD** ▶ As you read lines 146–179, continue to cite textual evidence.

- Underline the reasons given for Rwanda's failure.
- Circle the biggest failure that led to the genocide.
- Underline the reasons Rusesabagina gives for his actions.

less than a hotel manager, trained to negotiate contracts and charged to give shelter to those who need it. My job did not change in the genocide, even though I was thrust into a sea of fire. I only spoke the words that seemed normal and sane to me. I did what I believed to be the ordinary things that an ordinary man would do. I said no to outrageous actions the way I thought that anybody would, and it still mystifies me that so many others could say yes.

10. **◀ REREAD** Reread lines 158–160. What does Rusesabagina mean when he says that words are powerful tools of life, that they "may be the only ones"?

_____

_____

_____

_____

SHORT RESPONSE

Cite Text Evidence What is Rusesabagina's purpose in writing his book? What is the significance of the book's title, *An Ordinary Man*? Be sure to review your reading notes and **cite text evidence** in your response.

_____

_____

_____

_____

_____

_____

_____

_____

_____

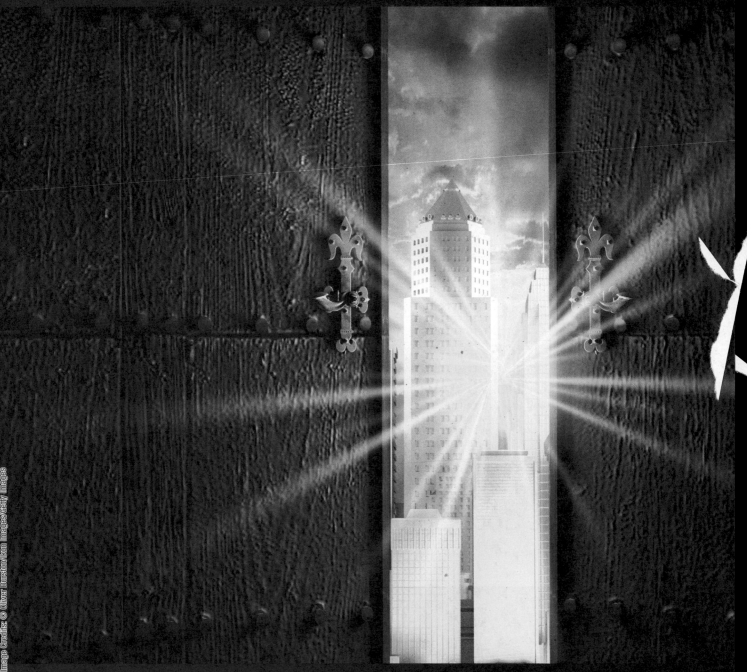

Heroes and Quests

Heroes and Quests

"If a journey doesn't have something to teach you about yourself, then what kind of journey is it?"

—Kira Salak

Background *No one knows for sure who* **Homer** *was, though the later Greeks believed he was a blind minstrel, or singer, who went from town to town. He is commonly credited with composing the* Iliad *(the story of the Trojan War) and the* Odyssey. *The Odyssey tells of the many adventures of a soldier named Odysseus on his ten-year journey home from the Trojan War. As this passage begins, Odysseus tells the story of encountering Polyphemus, the Cyclops.*

from the Odyssey
The Cyclops

Epic Poem by Homer   Translated by Robert Fitzgerald

CLOSE READ
Notes

1. **READ ▶** As you read lines 1–20, begin to collect and cite text evidence.

   • Underline text that reveals Odysseus's values.
   • In the margin, summarize his description of the Cyclopes.
   • Circle Odysseus's purpose for approaching the Cyclopes's island.

"In the next land we found were Cyclopes,[1]
giants, **louts**, without a law to bless them.   lout:
In ignorance leaving the fruitage of the earth in mystery
to the immortal gods, they neither plow
5   nor sow by hand, nor till the ground, though grain—
wild wheat and barley—grows untended, and
wine-grapes, in clusters, ripen in heaven's rain.
Cyclopes have no muster and no meeting,
no consultation or old tribal ways,
10 but each one dwells in his own mountain cave
dealing out rough justice to wife and child,
indifferent to what the others do. . . . "

---

[1] **Cyclopes:** refers to the creatures in plural; *Cyclops* is singular.

CLOSE READ
Notes

Across the bay from the land of the Cyclopes was a lush, deserted island.
Odysseus and his crew landed on the island in a dense fog and spent days
feasting on wine and wild goats and observing the mainland, where the
Cyclopes lived. On the third day, Odysseus and his company of men set out
to learn if the Cyclopes were friends or foes.

"When the young Dawn with finger tips of rose
came in the east, I called my men together
15 and made a speech to them:

> 'Old shipmates, friends,
the rest of you stand by; I'll make the crossing
in my own ship, with my own company,
and find out what the mainland natives are—
for they may be wild savages, and lawless,
20 or **hospitable** and god fearing men.'

hospitable:

At this I went aboard, and gave the word
to cast off by the stern. My oarsmen followed,
filing in to their benches by the rowlocks,
and all in line dipped oars in the gray sea.

25 As we rowed on, and nearer to the mainland,
at one end of the bay, we saw a cavern
yawning above the water, screened with laurel,
and many rams and goats about the place
inside a sheepfold—made from slabs of stone

---

2. ◀ **REREAD** Reread lines 1–20. Based on the text, what inferences can
you make about the values of Odysseus and his audience?

_____

_____

_____

---

3. **READ** ▶ As you read lines 21–60, continue to cite textual evidence.

- Underline text describing what Odysseus sees as he approaches land.
- Circle words Odysseus uses to describe the Cyclops.
- In the margin, explain what Odysseus brings with him to the island (lines
  41–60).

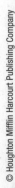

30   earthfast[2] between tall trunks of pine and rugged
      towering oak trees.

A prodigious man

      slept in this cave alone, and took his flocks
      to graze afield—remote from all companions,
      knowing none but savage ways, a brute
35   so huge, he seemed no man at all of those
      who eat good wheaten bread; but he seemed rather
      a shaggy mountain reared in solitude.
      We beached there, and I told the crew
      to stand by and keep watch over the ship;
40   as for myself I took my twelve best fighters
      and went ahead. I had a goatskin full
      of that sweet liquor that Euanthes'[3] son,
      Maron, had given me. He kept Apollo's
      holy grove at Ismarus; for kindness
45   we showed him there, and showed his wife and child,
      he gave me seven shining golden talents[4]
      perfectly formed, a solid silver winebowl,
      and then this liquor—twelve two-handled jars
      of brandy, pure and fiery. Not a slave
50   in Maron's household knew this drink; only
      he, his wife and the storeroom mistress knew;
      and they would put one cupful—ruby-colored,
      honey-smooth—in twenty more of water,
      but still the sweet scent hovered like a fume
55   over the winebowl. No man turned away
      when cups of this came round.

A wineskin full

      I brought along, and victuals in a bag,
      for in my bones I knew some towering brute
      would be upon us soon—all outward power,
60   a wild man, ignorant of civility.

      We climbed, then, briskly to the cave. But Cyclops
      had gone afield, to pasture his fat sheep,
      so we looked round at everything inside:

prodigious:

victuals:

---

[2] **earthfast:** firmly grounded.
[3] **Euanthes:** a god in Greek mythology.
[4] **talents:** bars of gold or silver of a specified weight, used as money in ancient Greece.

a drying rack that sagged with cheeses, pens

65 crowded with lambs and kids, each in its class:
firstlings apart from middlings, and the 'dewdrops,'
or newborn lambkins, penned apart from both.
And vessels full of whey[5] were brimming there—
bowls of earthenware and pails for milking.

70 My men came pressing round me, pleading:

'Why not
take these cheeses, get them stowed, come back,
throw open all the pens, and make a run for it?
We'll drive the kids and lambs aboard. We say
put out again on good salt water!'

Ah,

75 how sound that was! Yet I refused. I wished
to see the caveman, what he had to offer—
no pretty sight, it turned out, for my friends.
We lit a fire, burnt an offering,
and took some cheese to eat; then sat in silence

80 around the embers, waiting. When he came
he had a load of dry boughs on his shoulder
to stoke his fire at suppertime. He dumped it
with a great crash into that hollow cave,
and we all scattered fast to the far wall.

---

[5] **whey:** the watery part of milk, which separates from the curds, or solid part, during the making of cheese.

---

4. **◄ REREAD** Reread lines 55–60. Why does Odysseus bring the liquor with him? Cite text evidence in your response.

_____

_____

_____

5. **READ ▷** As you read lines 61–135, continue to cite textual evidence.

• Underline text describing the "sound" request that Odysseus's men make.

• Circle text that shows heroic qualities of Odysseus.

• In the margin, explain the ancient Greek custom "to honor strangers" described in lines 115–120.

85 Then over the broad cavern floor he ushered
    the ewes he meant to milk. He left his rams
    and he-goats in the yard outside, and swung
    high overhead a slab of solid rock
    to close the cave. Two dozen four-wheeled wagons,
90 with heaving wagon teams, could not have stirred
    the tonnage of that rock from where he wedged it
    over the doorsill. Next he took his seat
    and milked his bleating ewes. A practiced job
    he made of it, giving each ewe her suckling;
95 thickened his milk, then, into curds and whey,
    sieved out the curds to drip in withy baskets,[6]
    and poured the whey to stand in bowls
    cooling until he drank it for his supper.
    When all these chores were done, he poked the fire,
100 heaping on brushwood. In the glare he saw us.

    'Strangers,' he said, 'who are you? And where from?
    What brings you here by sea ways—a fair traffic?[7]
    Or are you wandering rogues, who cast your lives
    like dice, and **ravage** other folk by sea?'

ravage:

105 We felt a pressure on our hearts, in dread
    of that deep rumble and that mighty man.
    But all the same I spoke up in reply:

    'We are from Troy, Achaeans, blown off course
    by shifting gales on the Great South Sea;
110 homeward bound, but taking routes and ways
    uncommon; so the will of Zeus would have it.
    We served under Agamemnon,[8] son of Atreus—
    the whole world knows what city
    he laid waste, what armies he destroyed.
115 It was our luck to come here; here we stand,
    beholden for your help, or any gifts
    you give—as custom is to honor strangers.
    We would entreat you, great Sir, have a care
    for the gods' courtesy; Zeus will avenge
120 the unoffending guest.'

---

[6] **withy baskets:** baskets made from twigs.

[7] **fair traffic:** honest trade.

[8] **Agamemnon:** Commander of the Greek armed forces in the Trojan War.

He answered this
from his brute chest, unmoved:

'You are a ninny,
or else you come from the other end of nowhere,
telling me, mind the gods! We Cyclopes
care not a whistle for your thundering Zeus

125 or all the gods in bliss; we have more force by far.
I would not let you go for fear of Zeus—
you or your friends—unless I had a whim to.
Tell me, where was it, now, you left your ship—
around the point, or down the shore, I wonder?'

130 He thought he'd find out, but I saw through this,
and answered with a ready lie:

'My ship?
Poseidon Lord, who sets the earth a-tremble,
broke it up on the rocks at your land's end.
A wind from seaward served him, drove us there.

135 We are survivors, these good men and I.'

Neither reply nor pity came from him,
but in one stride he clutched at my companions
and caught two in his hands like squirming puppies
to beat their brains out, spattering the floor.

140 Then he dismembered them and made his meal,
gaping and crunching like a mountain lion—
everything: innards, flesh, and marrow bones.
We cried aloud, lifting our hands to Zeus,
powerless, looking on at this, appalled;

6. ◀ **REREAD AND DISCUSS** Reread lines 122–127. With a small group,
discuss the Cyclops's response to Odysseus's reminder to be hospitable
and not anger Zeus. What does this response tell you about the
Cyclops's attitude toward the gods?

7. **READ** ▶ As you read lines 136–244, continue to cite text evidence.

   • In the margin, explain Odysseus's reasoning in lines 148–154.
   • Circle the epithet, or repeated descriptive phrase, in line 156. Explain the
     meaning of these words in the margin.
   • Underline text that outlines Odysseus's plan in lines 170–244.

145   but Cyclops went on filling up his belly
with manflesh and great gulps of whey,
then lay down like a mast among his sheep.
My heart beat high now at the chance of action,
and drawing the sharp sword from my hip I went
150   along his flank to stab him where the midriff
holds the liver. I had touched the spot
when sudden fear stayed me: if I killed him
we perished there as well, for we could never
move his **ponderous** doorway slab aside.
155   So we were left to groan and wait for morning.

ponderous:

When the young Dawn with fingertips of rose
lit up the world, the Cyclops built a fire
and milked his handsome ewes, all in due order,
putting the sucklings to the mothers. Then,
160   his chores being all dispatched, he caught
another brace of men to make his breakfast,
and whisked away his great door slab
to let his sheep go through—but he, behind,
reset the stone as one would cap a quiver.
165   There was a din of whistling as the Cyclops
rounded his flock to higher ground, then stillness.
And now I pondered how to hurt him worst,
if but Athena granted what I prayed for.
Here are the means I thought would serve my turn:

170   a club, or staff, lay there along the fold—
an olive tree, felled green and left to season
for Cyclops' hand. And it was like a mast
a lugger[9] of twenty oars, broad in the beam—
a deep-sea-going craft—might carry:
175   so long, so big around, it seemed. Now I
chopped out a six foot section of this pole
and set it down before my men, who scraped it;
and when they had it smooth, I hewed again
to make a stake with pointed end. I held this
180   in the fire's heart and turned it, toughening it,
then hid it, well back in the cavern, under
one of the dung piles in profusion there.

---

[9] **lugger:** a small, wide sailing ship.

Now came the time to toss for it: who ventured
along with me? whose hand could bear to thrust
185   and grind that spike in Cyclops' eye, when mild
sleep had mastered him? As luck would have it,
the men I would have chosen won the toss—
four strong men, and I made five as captain.

At evening came the shepherd with his flock,
190   his woolly flock. The rams as well, this time,
entered the cave: by some sheep-herding whim—
or a god's bidding—none were left outside.
He hefted his great boulder into place
and sat him down to milk the bleating ewes
195   in proper order, put the lambs to suck,
and swiftly ran through all his evening chores.
Then he caught two more men and feasted on them.
My moment was at hand, and I went forward
holding an ivy bowl of my dark drink,
200   looking up, saying:

                            'Cyclops, try some wine.
Here's liquor to wash down your scraps of men.
Taste it, and see the kind of drink we carried
under our planks. I meant it for an offering
if you would help us home. But you are mad,
205   unbearable, a bloody monster! After this,
will any other traveller come to see you?'

He seized and drained the bowl, and it went down
so fiery and smooth he called for more:

'Give me another, thank you kindly. Tell me,
210   how are you called? I'll make a gift will please you.
Even Cyclopes know the wine-grapes grow
out of grassland and loam in heaven's rain,
but here's a bit of nectar and ambrosia!'[10]

Three bowls I brought him, and he poured them down.
215   I saw the fuddle and flush[11] come over him,
then I sang out in cordial tones:

---

[10] **ambrosia:** food of the gods.
[11] **fuddle and flush:** the state of confusion and redness of the face caused by drinking
    alcohol.

'Cyclops,
you ask my honorable name? Remember
the gift you promised me, and I shall tell you.
My name is Nohbdy: mother, father, and friends,
220   everyone calls me Nohbdy.'

                         And he said:
'Nohbdy's my meat, then, after I eat his friends.
Others come first. There's a noble gift, now.'

Even as he spoke, he reeled and tumbled backward,
his great head lolling to one side: and sleep
225   took him like any creature. Drunk, hiccupping,
he dribbled streams of liquor and bits of men.

Now, by the gods, I drove my big hand spike
deep in the embers, charring it again,
and cheered my men along with battle talk
230   to keep their courage up: no quitting now.
The **pike** of olive, green though it had been,   **pike:**
reddened and glowed as if about to catch.
I drew it from the coals and my four fellows
gave me a hand, lugging it near the Cyclops
235   as more than natural force nerved them; straight
forward they sprinted, lifted it, and rammed it
deep in his crater eye, and I leaned on it
turning it as a shipwright turns a drill
in planking, having men below to swing
240   the two-handled strap that spins it in the groove.
So with our brand we bored that great eye socket
while blood ran out around the red hot bar.
Eyelid and lash were seared; the pierced ball
hissed broiling, and the roots popped.

---

8. ◀ **REREAD AND DISCUSS** Reread lines 214–244. In a small group,
    discuss why Odysseus tells the Cyclops his name is "Nohbdy" (line 219).
    What is Odysseus planning?

9. **READ** ▶ As you read lines 245–339, continue to cite textual evidence.

    • In the margin, explain the action in lines 245–269.
    • Underline text that describes Odysseus's escape plan.
    • In the margin, explain how Odysseus and his men escape (lines 319–334).

In a smithy[12]

245   one sees a white-hot axehead or an adze

plunged and wrung in a cold tub, screeching steam—

the way they make soft iron hale and hard—:

just so that eyeball hissed around the spike.

The Cyclops bellowed and the rock roared round him,

250   and we fell back in fear. Clawing his face

he tugged the bloody spike out of his eye,

threw it away, and his wild hands went groping;

then he set up a howl for Cyclopes

who lived in caves on windy peaks nearby.

255   Some heard him; and they came by divers[13] ways

to clump around outside and call:

'What ails you,

Polyphemus? Why do you cry so sore

in the starry night? You will not let us sleep.

Sure no man's driving off your flock? No man

260   has tricked you, ruined you?'

Out of the cave

the mammoth Polyphemus roared in answer:

'Nohbdy, Nohbdy's tricked me, Nohbdy's ruined me!'

To this rough shout they made a sage reply:

'Ah well, if nobody has played you foul

265   there in your lonely bed, we are no use in pain

given by great Zeus. Let it be your father,

Poseidon Lord, to whom you pray.'

So saying

they trailed away. And I was filled with laughter

to see how like a charm the name deceived them.

270   Now Cyclops, wheezing as the pain came on him,

fumbled to wrench away the great doorstone

and squatted in the breach with arms thrown wide

for any silly beast or man who bolted—

hoping somehow I might be such a fool.

275   But I kept thinking how to win the game:

death sat there huge; how could we slip away?

---

[12] **smithy:** blacksmith's shop.

[13] **divers:** diverse; various.

I drew on all my wits, and ran through tactics,

reasoning as a man will for dear life,

until a trick came—and it pleased me well.

280 The Cyclops' rams were handsome, fat, with heavy

fleeces, a dark violet.

                                    Three abreast

I tied them silently together, twining

cords of willow from the ogre's bed;

then slung a man under each middle one

285 to ride there safely, shielded left and right.

So three sheep could convey each man. I took

the woolliest ram, the choicest of the flock,

and hung myself under his kinky belly,

pulled up tight, with fingers twisted deep

290 in sheepskin ringlets for an iron grip.

So, breathing hard, we waited until morning.

When Dawn spread out her finger tips of rose

the rams began to stir, moving for pasture,

and peals of bleating echoed round the pens

295 where dams with udders full called for a milking.

Blinded, and sick with pain from his head wound,

the master stroked each ram, then let it pass,

but my men riding on the pectoral fleece[14]

the giant's blind hands blundering never found.

300 Last of them all my ram, the leader, came,

weighted by wool and me with my **meditations.**   meditations:

The Cyclops patted him, and then he said:

'Sweet cousin ram, why lag behind the rest

in the night cave? You never linger so,

305 but graze before them all, and go afar

to crop sweet grass, and take your stately way

leading along the streams, until at evening

---

[14] **fleece:** wool covering a sheep's chest.

---

10. ◀ **REREAD AND DISCUSS** Reread lines 275–315. With a small group, discuss
how Odysseus exemplifies an epic hero in these lines. Cite text evidence in your
discussion.

you run to be the first one in the fold.
Why, now, so far behind? Can you be grieving
310   over your Master's eye? That carrion rogue
and his accurst companions burnt it out
when he had conquered all my wits with wine.
Nohbdy will not get out alive, I swear.
Oh, had you brain and voice to tell
315   where he may be now, dodging all my fury!
Bashed by this hand and bashed on this rock wall
his brains would strew the floor, and I should have
rest from the outrage Nohbdy worked upon me.'

He sent us into the open, then. Close by,
320   I dropped and rolled clear of the ram's belly,
going this way and that to untie the men.
With many glances back, we rounded up
his fat, stiff-legged sheep to take aboard,
and drove them down to where the good ship lay.
325   We saw, as we came near, our fellows' faces
shining; then we saw them turn to grief
tallying those who had not fled from death.
I hushed them, jerking head and eyebrows up,
and in a low voice told them: 'Load this herd;
330   move fast, and put the ship's head toward the breakers.'
They all pitched in at loading, then embarked
and struck their oars into the sea. Far out,
as far off shore as shouted words would carry,
I sent a few back to the adversary:

335   'O Cyclops! Would you feast on my companions?
Puny, am I, in a Caveman's hands?
How do you like the beating that we gave you,
you damned cannibal? Eater of guests
under your roof! Zeus and the gods have paid you!'

---

11. **READ ▶** As you read lines 340–404, continue to cite textual evidence.

- Underline text describing what Polyphemus does when he realizes Odysseus and his men have escaped and explain it in the margin (lines 340–352).
- Circle the protests made by Odysseus's crew.
- In the margin, paraphrase lines 366–375.

> ## " The blind thing in his doubled fury broke a hilltop in his hands and heaved it after us. "

340 The blind thing in his doubled fury broke
 a hilltop in his hands and heaved it after us.
 Ahead of our black prow it struck and sank
 whelmed in a spuming geyser, a giant wave
 that washed the ship stern foremost back to shore.
345 I got the longest boathook out and stood
 fending us off, with furious nods to all
 to put their backs into a racing stroke—
 row, row, or perish. So the long oars bent
 kicking the foam sternward, making head
350 until we drew away, and twice as far.
 Now when I cupped my hands I heard the crew
 in low voices protesting:

        'Godsake, Captain!
 Why bait the beast again? Let him alone!'
 'That tidal wave he made on the first throw
355 all but beached us.'

         'All but stove us in!'
 'Give him our bearing with your trumpeting,
 he'll get the range and lob a boulder.'

            'Aye
 He'll smash our timbers and our heads together!'
 I would not heed them in my glorying spirit,
360 but let my anger flare and yelled:

          'Cyclops,
 if ever mortal man inquire

how you were put to shame and blinded, tell him
Odysseus, raider of cities, took your eye:
Laertes'[15] son, whose home's on Ithaca!'

365   At this he gave a mighty sob and rumbled:

'Now comes the weird upon me, spoken of old.
A wizard, grand and wondrous, lived here—Telemus,[16]
a son of Eurymus; great length of days
he had in wizardry among the Cyclopes,
370   and these things he foretold for time to come:
my great eye lost, and at Odysseus' hands.
Always I had in mind some giant, armed
in giant force, would come against me here.
But this, but you—small, pitiful and twiggy—
375   you put me down with wine, you blinded me.
Come back, Odysseus, and I'll treat you well,
praying the god of earthquake to befriend you—
his son I am, for he by his avowal[17]
fathered me, and, if he will, he may
380   heal me of this black wound—he and no other
of all the happy gods or mortal men.'

Few words I shouted in reply to him:
'If I could take your life I would and take
your time away, and hurl you down to hell!
385   The god of earthquake could not heal you there!'

At this he stretched his hands out in his darkness
toward the sky of stars, and prayed Poseidon:
'O hear me, lord, blue girdler of the islands,
if I am thine indeed, and thou art father:
390   grant that Odysseus, raider of cities, never
see his home: Laertes' son, I mean,
who kept his hall on Ithaca. Should destiny
intend that he shall see his roof again
among his family in his father land,
395   far be that day, and dark the years between.

---

[15] **Laertes:** King of Ithaca, an island in the Ionian Sea.
[16] **Telemus:** a prophet in Greek mythology.
[17] **avowal:** honest admission.

Let him lose all companions, and return
under strange sail to bitter days at home.'
In these words he prayed, and the god heard him.
Now he laid hands upon a bigger stone

400 and wheeled around, titanic for the cast,
to let it fly in the black-prowed vessel's track.
But it fell short, just aft the steering oar,
and whelming seas rose giant above the stone
to bear us onward toward the island.

                                                     There

405 as we ran in we saw the squadron waiting,
the trim ships drawn up side by side, and all
our troubled friends who waited, looking seaward.
We beached her, grinding keel in the soft sand,
and waded in, ourselves, on the sandy beach.

410 Then we unloaded all the Cyclops' flock
to make division, share and share alike,
only my fighters voted that my ram,
the prize of all, should go to me. I slew him
by the sea side and burnt his long thighbones

415 to Zeus beyond the stormcloud, Cronus' son,
who rules the world. But Zeus disdained my offering;
destruction for my ships he had in store
and death for those who sailed them, my companions.

Now all day long until the sun went down
420 we made our feast on mutton and sweet wine,

---

12. **◄ REREAD** Reread ines 386–404. Explain Polyphemus's curse in your
own words.

_____

_____

_____

_____

13. **READ ▶** Read lines 405–429. Underline text foreshadowing future
events. In the margin, explain how the text "Zeus disdained my offering"
furthers the plot (line 416).

till after sunset in the gathering dark
we went to sleep above the wash of ripples.

When the young Dawn with finger tips of rose
touched the world, I roused the men, gave orders
425 to man the ships, cast off the mooring lines;
and filing in to sit beside the rowlocks
oarsmen in line dipped oars in the gray sea.
So we moved out, sad in the vast offing,[18]
having our precious lives, but not our friends."

---

[18] **offing:** the part of the deep sea seen from the shore.

14. ◀ **REREAD AND DISCUSS** Reread lines 423–429. With a small group, discuss why Odysseus and his men have mixed feelings as they leave the land of the Cyclopes.

SHORT RESPONSE

Cite Text Evidence In what ways is Odysseus an epic hero? Discuss his strengths and his flaws. Review your reading notes, and **cite text evidence** in your response.

_____

_____

_____

_____

_____

_____

_____

_____

_____

Background *In 2007, President Bush announced a new strategy for the war in Iraq known as "the surge." Many Americans were skeptical about sending even more American forces overseas. Among the troops sent to Baghdad was the Second Battalion, 16th Infantry under the command of Lieutenant Colonel Ralph Kauzlarich. Reporter* **David Finkel** *embedded with this battalion for eight months, reporting from the front lines. His book,* The Good Soldiers, *tells the stories of the men from this battalion and the families they left behind.*

from
The Good Soldiers

Nonfiction by David Finkel

CLOSE READ
Notes

1. **READD ▷** As you read lines 1–13, begin to collect and cite text evidence.

- Circle the central idea in lines 1–13.
- Underline details that support the central idea.
- In the margin, make an inference about Kauzlarich's faith in Izzy.

If Kauzlarich were to pick a favorite among the Iraqis he had met, Qasim[1] would be up there, and so would Mr. Timimi, the civil manager, who day after day did whatever he did in his office with the big desk and the broken cuckoo clock.

But Izzy, his interpreter, was the one Kauzlarich had grown closest to and who had come to represent all the reasons Kauzlarich continued to find faith in the goodness of Iraqis, even after eleven deaths. Six years older than Kauzlarich, Izzy was a thin man with a melancholy face, the face of someone who understood life as something to be resigned to. At one point,

10 he had lived for a few years in New York City, as part of Iraq's delegation to the United Nations, which was when he became fluent in English. Now his job was to interpret everything said in Arabic to Kauzlarich, as well as what Kauzlarich wanted to say to Iraqis, no matter what it was.

---

[1] **Kauzlarich, Qasim:** Lieutenant Colonel Ralph Kauzlarich, head of the 2-16 battalion. Colonel Qasim Ibrahim Alwan, head of a National Police battalion of Iraqis.

> ## "He was standing on a street with his bleeding daughter at his side."

There were times when Iraqis would look at Izzy in obvious disgust, as if he were nothing more than a tool of the Americans. But he did his job enthusiastically, partly because of his affection for the United States—his older daughter, now seventeen, was born in New York City—and partly because of something that had happened over the summer when he had gone home to spend a few days with his family in central Baghdad.

20   Late one afternoon, a bomb had exploded just outside of his apartment building. Even by Baghdad standards it was a monstrous explosion. Twenty-five people died and more than one hundred others were injured, but seven miles away, no one on the FOB[2] knew anything about it until Brent Cummings's[3] cell phone rang and Izzy was on the other end, in a panic.

There had been an explosion, he said. His apartment was in ruins, his building was on fire, and one of his daughters had been badly injured by

---

[2] **FOB:** an abbreviation for Forward Operations Base, a base set up in special operations to support training or tactical operations.

[3] **Brent Cummings:** Major Brent Cummings, Kauzlarich's second in command.

---

2. ◀ **REREAD**   Reread lines 5–13. What is the author's purpose in explaining Kauzlarich's feelings about Izzy? Support your answer with explicit text evidence.

_____

_____

_____

3. **READ** ▶   As your read lines 14–31, continue to cite text evidence.

• Underline the text in lines 14–19 that hints at an important event.

• In the margin, make an inference about some Iraqi attitudes toward Americans (lines14–19).

• Circle the central idea that describes Izzy's situation in lines 25–31.

something that had pierced her head. He had taken her to a hospital, but there were so many other injured people that doctors had said there was nothing they could do, that she needed more help than they could give, and

30 so he was standing on a street with his bleeding daughter at his side, afraid that she was going to die.

"The only hope you have is to get her to an American hospital?" Cummings asked, repeating what Izzy had just said. Izzy started to answer. The cell phone went dead. "Izzy?" Cummings said. "Izzy?"

How did moments of decency occur in this war?

"Izzy," Cummings said, calling him back. "Bring your daughter here." That was how.

"Oh thank you, sir. Thank you, sir," Izzy said.

And that's when things got complicated. Even this war had its rules,

40 and one of them covered who could be treated at an American aid facility. Americans could, of course, but Iraqis could not, unless they were injured by the American military, and only if the injury was life-threatening. Since the car bomb had been an Iraqi bomb, none of the injured was entitled to American care, including, it seemed, Izzy's daughter.

---

4. ◀ REREAD Reread lines 20–31. How does the author develop the sense that events are unfolding quickly? Support your answer with explicit textual evidence.

_____

_____

_____

_____

_____

_____

_____

5. READ ▶ As you read lines 32–49, continue to cite textual evidence.

- In the margin, explain what Cummings tells Izzy to do.
- Circle the author's reflections in lines 31–39.
- In the margin, explain the reasoning behind the author's thoughts.

But Cummings had in mind Izzy's previous life, before he was an interpreter. If the daughter who was injured had been born in New York City, did that make her eligible? Could an American-born Iraqi who was injured by a non-American bomb receive medical care in an American military medical facility?

50   Cummings didn't know the answer. He phoned some doctors at the aid station, but they didn't know, either. He tried the FOB legal representative, but couldn't get through. He wasn't even sure which of the daughters had been injured—the one born in New York, or the eight-year-old who was born in Baghdad. He called Izzy back. The connection was terrible. He dialed again and again.

"Izzy . . . okay . . . where is your daughter that is from the United States?"

Again the phone went dead.

He called again. The connection kept breaking up. "Is your daughter

60 from the United States with you right now? . . . Is she hurt? . . . Which daughter is hurt? . . . Is she on the street with you? . . . You can't what? . . . What?"

Again the phone went dead, and at that point Cummings made a decision not to ask any more questions, just to assume what the answer would be. He was making a guess. He understood that. But with Kauzlarich

---

6. ◀ **REREAD** Reread lines 32–49. Explain Izzy's dilemma. Why does the author pose two questions in lines 45–49?

_____

_____

_____

_____

7. ▶ **READ** As you read lines 50–67, continue to cite textual evidence.

- Circle each use of "didn't know" in lines 50–55. In the margin, explain how this repetition highlights the conflict.

- Underline the decision Cummings makes in lines 63–67. In the margin, draw an inference as to why he makes that decision.

away for a few hours on another FOB to attend a memorial ceremony, there was no one else to ask what to do.

He telephoned an officer in another battalion who controlled access to the FOB and whose approval would be needed for someone not in the 70 military to get through the gate without being turned away, detained, or shot. "Yes," he said. "I'm sure we can produce a birth certificate." He wondered whether such a certificate, if it even existed, had burned up in the fire. He checked the time. The sun was going down. A curfew would be in effect soon, at which point Izzy and his daughter wouldn't be allowed outside until sunrise. The officer kept asking questions. "We'll figure that piece out," Cummings said impatiently. "Right now, I just want to help the guy."

Next he called the battalion's physician and told him to be ready to treat one female, age unknown, in a matter of minutes. "A U.S. citizen," he 80 added, and then to that added, "maybe."

Next he tried Izzy again, to see how close he was to the FOB, and Izzy, his voice more panicked than before, said he wasn't close at all, that he was still on the street, still next to his daughter, trying to find a taxi. "Thank you, sir," he kept saying. "Thank you, sir. Thank you, sir."

There was nothing to do but wait. It wasn't as if a convoy could go pick up Izzy. He would have to get here on his own. The sun was almost down

8. ◄ REREAD Reread lines 56–62. How do the short, choppy lines of dialogue affect the pacing of the narrative? Support your answer with explicit textual evidence.

_____

_____

_____

_____

9. READ ▶ As you read lines 68–129, continue to cite textual evidence.

• Underline every mention of a call made by or answered by Cummings.
• Circle statements Cummings makes that may not be true.
• Underline text explaining what Cummings knows when he sees Izzy and his family.

now. A call came from an officer in another battalion who said he'd heard that the 2-16 had lost some soldiers somewhere. "No," Cummings said. Then another officer called saying he'd heard some soldiers had been

90 injured in an apartment bombing. Then another: the rumor was that some 2-16 soldiers had died in an EFP[4] attack.

"No, there are no injured Coalition Forces,"[5] Cummings kept saying. "It is an Iraqi—an Iraqi American—who was hurt. It is the interpreter's daughter."

He phoned Izzy again.

Still trying to find a taxi.

Another call, from the doctor: "I don't know the extent of the injuries . . . I don't know if he's even in a cab yet . . . I don't know if they're going to make it here before curfew."

100 Another call. It was Izzy. They were in a taxi. They were on the bridge, two minutes from the base.

Cummings hurried to the gate. It was dark now. The FOB's ambulance pulled up to receive the girl. Five minutes had gone by. Where was the taxi? Now the guards said they had stopped it in the distance and that there was no way it would be allowed any closer than it had gotten, which was somewhere out of sight. "Get a litter," Cummings yelled to the ambulance crew. Sprinting, he went out the gate, passing coils of razor wire and blast walls, and then stopping when he saw Izzy walking toward him, illuminated by the headlights of the ambulance.

110 Izzy's clothing was filthy.

Next to him was his wife, who was crying.

On his other side was one of his daughters, the one born in New York, who appeared to be uninjured.

And in front of them all, wobbly but walking, was a young girl with shiny purple sandals, blood all over her blue jeans, and a bandage covering the left side of her face.

It was the eight-year-old, the daughter born in Baghdad, the one who according to the rules had no standing whatsoever to be treated on the FOB. "Izzy," Cummings called out, knowing right then that he had guessed

120 wrong. He ran toward the family as other soldiers reached the girl. They lifted her up. She began crying. They carried her through the gate without stopping. They ran with her into the aid station, and as the doors swung

---

[4] **EFP:** Explosively Formed Penetrator, also known as Explosively Formed Projectile, a warhead designed to penetrate armor.

[5] **Coalition Forces:** military command led by the United States and its allies during the Iraq War.

> **"** . . . when he was unable to say anything else, he bowed his head, and then wiped his eyes . . . **"**

shut she cried out in Arabic for her father, who'd been told to remain in the lobby.

Izzy took a seat in a corner. Cummings stood nearby. "Was it a car bomb?" he asked after a while.

"No, sir," Izzy said. "It was two car bombs."

And then he said nothing more, not until one of the doctors came into the lobby to tell him that his daughter was going to be all right.

130   "Thank you, sir," he managed to say, and when he was unable to say anything else, he bowed his head, and then wiped his eyes, and then followed the doctor into the treatment area, where he saw his Iraqi daughter surrounded by American doctors and medics.

What do the rules say?

At that moment, anyway, no one seemed concerned one way or another: not the doctors, not the family, and not Cummings, who stood at the very same spot he'd stood at as he watched Crow[6] die, watching once again.

The injuries to the girl were serious. There was a deep cut across her cheek, and worse, something had gone into the left side of her forehead, near her temple, and was deeply embedded in bone. Izzy held her hand as the doctors wrapped her in a sheet, making sure to secure her arms tightly.

---

[6] **Crow:** Sergeant William Crow died from an EFP hit on his convoy in June 2007.

---

10. ◀ **REREAD AND DISCUSS**   With a small group, discuss whether or not you think Cummings made the right decision.

11. **READ** ▶   As you read lines 130–152, continue to cite textual evidence.

- Circle the question the author asks.
- Underline text describing similarities between the Americans and the Iraqis.
- In the margin, explain a possible theme of lines 130–137.

Her mother closed her eyes. The doctors leaned in. It took a while, and at the worst of it the little girl couldn't remain quiet, but then the doctors were showing her what they had pulled out—a thick piece of glass nearly two inches long.

The glass had been part of an apartment that no longer existed, in a section of Baghdad where the sounds that night were of mourning.

150 But here on the FOB, the sounds were of a mother whose home was ruined kissing her daughter's face, and a father whose home was ruined kissing his daughter's hand, and a little girl whose home was ruined saying something in Arabic that caused her family to smile, and Cummings saying quietly in English, "Man, I haven't felt this good since I got to this hellhole."

12. **◀ REREAD** Reread lines 146–152. In the margin, compare the sounds described in these lines. What mood does each create?

SHORT RESPONSE

Cite Text Evidence   What is the central idea of this piece? Explain how the author introduces and develops that idea over the course of the text. Review your reading notes and **cite text evidence**.

_____

_____

_____

_____

_____

_____

_____

_____

_____

_____

Acknowledgments

"And of Clay Are We Created" from *The Stories of Eva Luna* by Isabel Allende. Text copyright © 1989 by Isabel Allende. English translation copyright © 1991 by Macmillan Publishing Company. Reprinted by permission of Simon & Schuster, Inc. and Agencia Literaria Carmen Balcells.

Excerpt from *Animals in Translation: Using the Mysteries of Autism to Decode Animal Behavior* by Temple Grandin and Catherine Johnson. Text copyright © 2005 by Temple Grandin and Catherine Johnson. Reprinted by permission of Simon & Schuster, Inc. and Betsy Lerner.

Excerpt from *The Good Soldiers* by David Finkel. Text copyright © 2009 by David Finkel. Reprinted by permission of Farrar, Straus and Giroux, LLC, The Melanie Jackson Agency and Atlantic Books.

Excerpt from "Introduction: Love's Vocabulary" from *A Natural History of Love* by Diane Ackerman. Text copyright © 1994 by Diane Ackerman. Reprinted by permission of Random House, Inc. Any third party use of this material, outside of this publication, is prohibited. Interested parties must apply directly to Random House, Inc. for permission.

"Making the Future Better Together" (retitled from "After September 11, 2011, Focus on the Next 10 Years") by Eboo Patel from *The Washington Post*, September 12, 2011. Text copyright © 2011 by Eboo Patel. Reprinted by permission of Eboo Patel.

"Marie Colvin: 'Our mission is to report these horrors of war with accuracy and without prejudice'" by Marie Colvin from *The Guardian*, February 22, 2012, www.guardian.co.uk. Text copyright © by Marie Colvin. Reprinted by permission of the Estate of Marie Colvin.

"My Ceremony for Taking" by Lara Mann from *www.drunkenboat.com*, November 15, 2012. Text copyright © 2012 by Lara Mann. Reprinted by permission of Drunken Boat.

"Night Calls" by Lisa Fugard from *Outside*, Vol. xx, No. 5, May 1995. Text copyright © 1995 by Lisa Fugard. Reprinted by permission of Lisa Fugard.

Excerpts from *The Odyssey* by Homer, translated by Robert Fitzgerald. Translation copyright © 1961, 1963 by Robert Fitzgerald, renewed © 1989 by Benedict R.C. Fitzgerald on behalf of the Fitzgerald children. Reprinted by permission of Farrar, Straus and Giroux, LLC and Benedict Fitzgerald.

Excerpt from "Introduction" from *An Ordinary Man: An Autobiography* by Paul Rusesabagina, with Tom Zoellner. Text copyright © 2006 by Paul Rusesabagina. Reprinted by permission of Viking Penguin, a division of Penguin Group (USA) Inc.

"The Prisoner Who Wore Glasses" from *Tales of Tenderness and Power* by Bessie Head. Text copyright © 1989 by The Estate of Bessie Head. Reprinted by permission of Johnson & Alcock.

"The Stayer" from *Palm Crows* by Virgil Suárez. Text copyright © 2001 by Virgil Suárez. Reprinted by permission of The University of Arizona Press.

"The Survivor" from *The Phoenix Gone, The Terrace Empty* by Marilyn Chin. Text copyright © 1994 by Marilyn Chin. Reproduced with permission of Milkweed Editions.

Excerpt from "What Can I Do to Make Things Better" by Kofi Annan from *Parade Magazine*. Text copyright © by Kofi Annan. Reprinted by permission of Kofi Annan.

"Who Understands Me But Me" from *Immigrants in Our Own Land* by Jimmy Santiago Baca. Text copyright © 1977, 1979, 1981, 1982, 1990 by Jimmy Santiago Baca. Reprinted by permission of New Directions Publishing Corporation.

Index of Titles & Authors